How Do I Know You?

A Caregiver's Lifesaver for Dealing with Dementia

By

C. Charlotte Bishop, MS, GCM, CRC, CCM, LCPC

and Steven R. Steiber, PhD

Your Caregiver's Lifesaver ™ vol. 1

How Do I Know You?

A Caregiver's Lifesaver for Dealing with Dementia

By

C. Charlotte Bishop, MS, GCM, CRC, CCM, LCPC

and Steven R. Steiber, PhD

Family Solutions Press

Los Angeles, California

"...your insight and expertise...It's wonderful to know that there are people available to navigate these very difficult and complicated issues."

Suzanne

"You became a part of my family that I never expected...I am truly thankful." Mary

PREFACE

"I don't remember." "Who are you?" "I forgot." A colleague of ours talks of the 20+ calls he'd get from his mom every day. It was a new call each time for his mom, but it inevitably was the same issue for him. It got to the point he would just freeze, a knot in his stomach, when he saw his mother's phone number on his cell screen. It was Ground Hog Day EVERY day... or Steve's mom's favorite go to phrase when introducing him to her friends was "you don't have a name. Let me introduce you to my son." It's what we call "covering"...a way that people who are suffering from early stage dementia cope with living in the fog that has become "their world." As care managers we hear these every day. Do you?

Sound familiar? If so, you are not alone. We estimate that in excess of 8 million Americans have some form of dementia, and that means there may be twice that many people in your shoes trying to figure out what to do about the increasing demands of caring for mom or dad or your wife or your husband or other loved one. As a caregiver to a loved one with dementia, it can wear you down, stress you, worry you and make you sad. It may create a financial hardship for you or your loved one. You may have difficulty sleeping, getting to work on time or focusing on work. It can become your other full-time job. And it can burn you out!

How do you know the good options for caring for your loved one with dementia? We are the professionals who can help you navigate the path to the "good options." We are often called care managers or care navigators. We also interviewed 30 other professional care managers across the United States and compiled 350 case studies on how care managers help caregivers figure things out. Seventy of those case studies were specifically about families dealing with dementia. Getting a plan with the right options helped caregivers like you to be less worn down, less stressed, less worried, less sad and more in control.

This book focuses on what we know that can be your lifesaver to ease your pain and help you find the best way to address your problems. It also will help you to care for you, the caregiver. There is no "one size fits all" plan, but we think you will find parts of your plan in the case studies we share in this short book. The key to peace of mind is to have a plan, even if you have to make adjustments along the way. Let us be your companion and guide as you navigate this challenging time of life for your parents or your spouse or yourself.

TABLE OF CONTENTS

INTRODUCTION

Congratulations. You have come so far to get here. Let us help you navigate the path from here forward, or if feel you are going under, let us throw you a lifesaver. A family crisis does not make an appointment; it just shows up. One in three family crises with an older loved one will be created by the onset of dementia in the family. If you are among this one in three, you now are a second responder to your family crisis, and whether you had made plans for it or not, we are here to work with you. It is our intent to not just inform you about what dementia is (perhaps more appropriately since there are nearly one hundred manifestations under the label dementia) ... what dementias are. We will be sharing with you some real life examples of other families and their experiences when dementia visits the family. And despite the fact that we are professional care managers, it is not just our experience we are putting to paper here. We have tapped into the experiences of three dozen professional care managers from across the country to give you the benefit of their collective training and work experience.

ABOUT THE AUTHORS

Charlotte Bishop is a certified Aging Life Care Professional with a Master's degree in rehabilitation along with four other professional certifications that reinforce her credentials as a care manager.   Her personal and professional experiences have formed her opinion that a family catastrophe does not make an appointment, you have to be ready when it shows up. Consequently, she specializes in helping families anticipate and prepare for challenging medical, personal, residential and environmental issues for themselves or aging family members as well as cope with the crises when they happen.

Extensive experience in medical management for individuals with a variety of diagnoses and life situations has enabled Ms. Bishop to be the lifesaver for countless caregivers. Ms. Bishop's knowledge of community resources and her ability to navigate complex care plans enhance the effectiveness of her efforts. This personal and professional journey has been the beginning of the part of **CCM** dedicated to "*Serving Elders and Others with Special Needs*" – now called **Creative Care Management**. **Creative Care Management** has grown to a team of certified professionals providing options to older adults and their families throughout metropolitan Chicago.

> *A 2014 survey of executives in U.S. Accountable Care Organizations covering 5.2 million lives under the Affordable Care Act said Care Managers were their most effective and important tool in reducing hospital readmissions.*

Steven Steiber, Ph.D. is Vice President with **Creative Care Management**, a position he has held since 2005. In that role, he acts as pharmaceutical consultant, corporate consulting liaison, chief marketing officer and first point of contact for new clients to **Creative Care Management**. He has his doctorate in behavioral science from the University of Arizona, and his writing has appeared in *The Journal of the American Medical Association*, *Public Opinion Quarterly*, *Social Forces*, *The American Journal of Public Health*, *Hospitals and Health Networks* and *Modern Healthcare* and more. He also has co-authored a book on *Measuring and Managing Patient Satisfaction* through American Hospital Publishing, which is in its second edition.

Dr. Steiber began his career with the Center for Health Policy of the American Medical Association. Following that, he has consulted with hospitals and other health care providers, professional associations and health insurers, senior residential communities and medical device and pharmaceutical manufacturers. He has personally interviewed thousands of physicians, nurses, pharmacists, opinion leaders and other health care professionals and executives as a consultant. His clients have included the American Hospital Association, the Illinois Hospital Association, State Farm Insurance, Classic Residence by Hyatt, Abbott Laboratories, Astra Zeneca, Eli Lilly, Merck and Company among many others.

PART ONE:

Caregiving in
the 21st Century

"For most of us, our formal education and other life experiences don't give us any information about crisis management, problem solving, or even problem recognition."

...Dr. Phil McGraw
Real Life: Preparing for the Seven Most Challenging Days of Your Life

---

Chapter One:

The scope of the "caregiver crisis"

Do you have a parent, an aunt, an uncle, a grandparent, or an older neighbor...an older loved one who is special to you? Are you over the age of 50? Then you and nearly 109 million other Americans are on the road toward a caregiver crisis. When you get that call that mom has fallen or dad was found wandering or your loved one has THAT diagnosis, it's going to feel like a roller coaster; but this particular ride can go off the rails.

> ***More than 95 million adult Americans
> are just a phone call away
> from being a caregiver
> to a parent or older loved one.***

Some caregivers make plans. But in a 2015 survey of caregivers, less than half said that they have an actual plan in place to help address the future needs of their older loved ones.

And only one in four of these felt their care plans were fully up to the task. So, seven in eight of the 109 million unprepared caregivers will need a lifesaver.

In a 2011 survey of working Americans by MetLife, nearly 10 million workers over the age of 50 were presently caring for an older parent enough hours per week that it had become like another job. The sum total of these overtime hours from caregivers that already have a day job is an industry that would be valued at $3 trillion dollars a year were they compensated for their time. The AARP Public Policy Institute reported in 2013 the number of unpaid caregivers to be closer to 40 million Americans. Their estimate of the value of the unpaid caregiving ballooned up to $470 billion. These are the 10 to 40 million people whose crises have arrived; the rest of the 60 to 100 million are on the road. When the crisis hits, the ride will be anything but smooth.

Employers talk about this caregiver crisis not just in terms of the days caregivers are taking from work in the form of absenteeism or family leave, but also in terms of the distractions to the workforce. It's the phone calls in the middle of the work shift, it's the on-line searches for home care for mom, it's the distraction by the weight of the added responsibilities that caregiving represents. These distractions have grown to such a scale that they now have a name; employers call is "presenteeism" ... a work productivity killer that equates these distracted workers as just one small step away from the absent workers. It has become a big enough issue in human resource circles that if you go to the web site for human resource managers (Society for Human Resource Management at www.shrm.org/searchcenter) and type "elder caregiver" in the search bar, you will get more than 90 results.

We talk about the unpredictable timing of caregiving as an imminent crisis. The crisis that AARP forecasts, however, is based on what they call the "caregiver support ratio" – the ratio of caregivers to care receivers. They project that this ratio will fall from 7.2 caregivers for each care receiver in 2010 to 2.9 caregivers to one in 2050. We come back again to not merely the numbers, but how ill-prepared today's and tomorrow's caregivers are. The one-third of Americans to whom we are speaking are those in an at risk category based on being potentially a younger caregiver to an older care receiver or being a caregiver to an aging spouse, partner or dear friend.

This book is based on the insights of the professionals who arguably are the "second responders" for the families of older adults at risk: care managers. These professionals have been called Geriatric Care Managers and more recently Aging Life Care Professionals (www.aginglifecare.org/ALCA). Care managers may be social workers, nurses, gerontologists or other human services professionals that focus on the needs of older individuals as well as their families in meeting the unique medical, environmental, social, psychological and financial challenges of aging. In addition to being in the business of care management ourselves, we interviewed more than three dozen Aging Life Care Professionals (Care Managers) across the United States about the families they serve, the incidents, accidents and diagnoses that bring them to the service of the caregiving family members and support of the care receiving elders. We asked them to help us do "grand rounds" on these engagements and share with us an understanding of what happens most often and what are the resources that can be brought to bear to support these networks of need. In the end, these care managers helped us digest the experiences and lessons learned across 350 case studies. While there are no "cookie cutter" approaches to a complex predicament such as what dementia presents to families whose elder may be manifesting the cognitive changes of a dementia diagnosis, there are some general learnings that can be used by families who have just received the diagnosis. There are steps that can be taken early on and all along the trajectory of this condition that will be beneficial to both the care receiver and their caregivers.

This book is based on some of the 350 case studies drawn from in-depth interviews with more than three dozen professional geriatric care managers.

In the business of care management ourselves, we interviewed more than three dozen Aging Life Care Professionals (Care Managers) across the United States about the families they serve, the incidents, accidents and diagnoses that bring them to the service of the caregiving family members and support of the care receiving elders. We asked them to help us do "grand rounds" on these engagements and share with us an understanding of what happens most often and what are the resources that can be brought to bear to support these networks of need. In the end, these care managers helped us digest the experiences and lessons learned across 350 case studies. While there are no "cookie cutter" approaches to a complex predicament such as what dementia presents to families whose elder may be manifesting the cognitive changes of a dementia diagnosis, there are some general learnings that can be used by families who have just received the diagnosis. There are steps that can be taken early on and all along the trajectory of this condition that will be beneficial to both the care receiver and their caregivers.

We are in the business of being the "second responders" that support families who have had the call or have spotted the crisis as it begins to rear its head. The adult children who notice the accumulation of spoiled food in the refrigerator when they are at their parents for Thanksgiving, the relative who gets five calls the same day from a parent who does not remember the first four calls about what they perceive to be some pressing need or another. The bruise on mom or dad that is not a sign of abuse but rather a warning sign of the first "small fall" that did not break a hip. We pay second responders, because we are not reached by a call to 911; if we had a number it would be 912.

> **Everyone knows who to call when there is an**
> **emergency, but whom do you call after**
> **the emergency is handled?**

But what prompted our interest in getting the word out to more people who will soon be losing sleep about what to do about mom, how to help dad who refuses help and how to support a proud older adult whose life has been defined by their self-sufficiency?   We came across a survey conducted by a consulting group interested in one of the emerging forms of managed care spawned by the Affordable Care Act, often referred to as Obamacare.   They had reached out to chief executives in Accountable Care Organizations, the CEOs, COOs, CFOs and CIOs. When asked what tools these executives have for reducing hospital readmissions for the people whose lives they insure, the majority voted that Professional Care Managers were both the most important and the most effective means for keeping a discharged patient from bouncing right back to a hospital. What they saw as important about care management was very much in step with our own experiences.   Care management makes health care more effective, but it also makes home safer, makes financial or legal navigation easier and in general just improves an older person's quality of life while it offers peace of mind to caregivers and other family members. This is bigger than a medical model; it is a quality of life model _and_ a medical model.

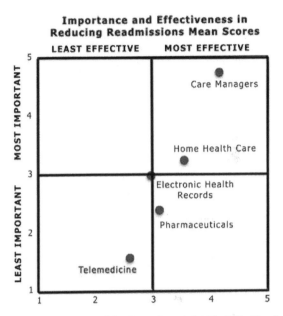

Importance and Effectiveness in Reducing Readmissions Mean Scores

2015 Accountable Care Organization Outlook
Future Implications for Suppliers and Providers

This book is <u>not</u> about what you should know if you want to be a Professional Care Manager; that would be a different level course. It is about what we have learned in our day jobs and what Care Managers whom we have interviewed do every day that everyone with an older loved one in their orbit can learn from. How can you learn to see what they see when they walk into a home to do a safety assessment? What questions do you need to ask at mom's or dad's next medical appointment to work more aggressively toward enhanced wellness? What do you need to know about an older loved one's consumer rights in a residential facility to advocate for better care? What are the conversations you need to start with a loved one that will enhance their safety and quality of life? What do you need to know to take some of the uncertainty and stress out of caregiving?

But it also gets personal. The founder of our company was thrust into the caregiving role with a phone call and a subsequent diagnosis of her husband's brain cancers...yes, there were two cancers. And then how to confront a terminal diagnosis and at the same time care for three dependent children, a home and a business. And as this book was being drafted, another of our team got the call from his sister. The independent living facility where their 90-year old mom was living quite happily had called to inform her as Power of Attorney that mom was to be evicted in thirty days as her needs now exceeded what their staff could provide under statutory guidelines. This book is about what you do after "The call."

Chapter Two:

Breaking some caregiver "myths"

> *A care plan is a bit like a military strategy:*
> *it changes pretty fast once*
> *the first shots are fired.*

Even if you are one of the estimated 15 million caregivers who already have what you feel to be an effective plan for your older loved one, we hope that you will find some added information and perspective in the pages that follow. The case studies on which we have built our recommendations for caregivers and their care receivers will have the most current information and some really insightful perspectives from the years of experience represented by the Care Managers with whom we have consulted. And if you are among the 95 million who have either no plan at all or a plan that you consider to be suboptimal, we will help you get up to speed as well. So, we will start at the beginning...with nine of the traps that can ensnare caregivers we have known as they cope with their aging, older loved ones.

<u>As your parent(s) age, you will reverse roles.</u>

One of the more common traps we see starts out with a variation on a theme of "reversing roles" as the parent ages and the adult children now become the de facto parents. "Now that my parents have gotten to be ___ years old," they may say, "we have switched roles and I will be taking care of them."

Let's be really clear. Just because your older loved one may ask you to drive them to an appointment does not mean they have invited you to be in the driver's seat of their lives. As an individual ages, they do lose some of the vigor of their younger selves. They do not, however, need to be parented.

> **You may be older, but you will never**
> **become your parents' parent.**

They may just need someone to listen to their complaint, not to "fix the problem." They may simply wish to have some help – and companionship – in a project, not someone to take over the controls. As one of our clients periodically observes after a particularly challenging day: I can still do all the things I used to do...just not all in the same day. An effective caregiver is one who knows how to listen, and when to ask the simple question: "Do you want me to help fix this, or do you want me to simply listen?"

1. *As you grow older – and your parent(s) age- you can get even.*

> **You cannot change your past with your parents, but you can help make both of your futures better.**

One of the faulty assumptions that we see acted out more often than given actual voice is in the form of an adult child who has carried a grudge from their early years. It is the long-festering rivalry that still comes out as, "You never gave me the same privileges you gave to _____." Maybe it manifests itself as harmlessly as a constant drive to show what they can achieve, can earn or can accumulate. Or it can be a more malicious act that seeks to get even with mom or dad through financial manipulation or even financial or physical abuse. We have seen it in the sibling arguments about what one child frames as using mom's financial resources to give mom a safe and comfortable life trajectory versus what another adult child perceives as squandering "their inheritance." It is important for the adult children who feel sufficiently aggrieved that they are spoiling to get even to remember that their growing children are watching their own mom or dad for cues on how one treats older parents. We have seen it devolve to everyone gets their own lawyers and the courts settle what the adults could not.

2. *Big sister will take care of the parents.*

And then there is the trap that both the older loved one and the adult children fashion for the older sister. Sister will take care of mom or dad...most often mom.

> *It's a fact that female caregivers outnumber male caregivers - not unlike females are the stay at home parent more than males.*

In an age with huge strides made by women in the labor force and in all manner of important professions, we have found this to be a little out of step. That is, until one also looks at a reasonable parallel in American patterns in child-rearing. Even with so many women with advanced degrees and their high rates of participation in the labor force, we have only to look at the relative numbers of fathers who are stay at home dads. The latest numbers suggest about one in six stay at home parents is the father, and the balance are mothers. So, it may not be a stretch to suggest that this also is a trap that the older sister has a hand in fashioning. We caution that attending to the needs of aging parents ought to be a matter for family conversation and consensus regardless of who ultimately takes the lead. It should not be a foregone conclusion that big sister is the best for the task or that she even chooses to shoulder the brunt of caregiving responsibilities.

3. *Leave the caregiving to the one who did not leave home.*

In a parallel vein, the sibling who did not leave the home town or the one who already is an at-home parent can be a default caregiver in some families. The local sibling may be closest geographically when a crisis occurs, and those who are "distance caregivers" may be fine with the default relegation of caregiving tasks to the local sib. In our experience, caregiving is much more than just geography and travel time. Any adult child to an older loved one who lives across town, has a full-time job, has a spouse or children or just has a life qualifies as a distance caregiver. Regardless of geography, today's caregivers can be anywhere and be doing just about anything and still play a support role for an older family member in need.

> *Distance caregiving is not so much about geography as it is about all the demands on adult children of older loved ones.*

Yesterday's technology – the telephone - still works to keep us in touch, but there is also an entire array of apps that enable a distance caregiver to check to see if mom or dad have gotten out of bed today, or left the house. They have an app that can tell you if mom or dad has opened their pill box after a prompt by an electronic reminder to take their meds. It may even send you a text or email when that happens. And yes, you can even

27

watch mom or dad in real time from your phone or computer with a signal generated by a camera in their home, but we have to emphasize here that all of these are with the older loved one's consent or the consent of the medical power of attorney. The power of attorney can kick in if the older loved one's judgments have become impaired or if their physical safety is considered to be at risk.

And let's not overlook good old-fashioned eyes and ears. We are strong supporters of the "village" when it comes to care for older loved ones. We've all heard that it takes a village to raise a child, but the same holds for looking after an older loved one. To some extent local friends of mom or dad can be extremely helpful as the people who can tell you how your older loved one is doing. For aging loved ones who need help with their activities of daily living, care also can be brought to their home by either home health or home care providers. This can range from just a few visits or hours a week to 24 hour care from a professional who is bonded and insured and trained in the care required for a care receiver's physical and mental needs. Bottom-line is that distance need not be the factor that relegates, or denies anyone, the role of caregiver.

4. *Google has an answer to everything.*

Welcome to the 21st century, an age in which you literally can Google anything. But that also is what you will find…just about anything, so how do you sort out the good from the bad from the ugly. How will you know? We are here to tell you that it is not by page ranking. In the chapters that follow, we will be providing useful web resources for the challenges you are most likely to face as a caregiver to an older loved one.

> **The best answers to your caregiving questions will not necessarily be what your search engine ranks at the top of the list.**

Most of these resources have a reputable professional association behind them vetting the solutions and answers they offer. And most also have searchable sites that will help you in finding reasonable and realistic options. When your crisis occurs you don't need someone making your decisions for you, but you will benefit from a reputable resource who can give you some options from which to choose.

5. *Doctor knows best.*

Physicians in their first week of medical school are imparted the wisdom of the Greek physician named Hippocrates who is attributed that four word principal: "First, do no harm." Perhaps these students would be well-advised to also follow Sherlock Holmes' famed dictum: "Assume nothing." Yet there are still too many who seem to fall into the trap that "doctor knows best;" physicians do know a lot, but the patients and the patients' families are key decision-makers. This is where "informed consent" comes into play. Physicians inform; patients and families decide. This is not going to be a book about medical mistakes, but a few demographic facts can help to paint a potentially frightening picture.

> ***Your parents' doctor can only be as good as the questions you ask.***

While the over 65 year set comprises only about 13 percent of the U.S. population, they account for about 30 percent of all prescriptions filled. And 65+ year olds are estimated to comprise between 40 and 50 percent of all over the counter medications sold each year. Nearly two of every five hospitalizations each year are the result of medication side effects or drug/drug interactions among older patients. Older adults represent fully half of all drug-related deaths each year.

It is important to appreciate that older adults are not just older versions of younger adults. They metabolize their medications more slowly, so dosing should be different not just based on their weight. Older adults tend to be markedly less hydrated which means they will eliminate drugs from their systems less efficiently than younger adults. And when drugs are tested for approval by the FDA, truly older adults or older adults with co-morbidities rarely are among the patients tested in the clinical trials. You may be aware that drugs to be used on young children must go through clinical trials among children within the specific age cohort before they receive approval for use in those populations. Only then can the drug be listed in the package insert that accompanies prescriptions. No such federal guidelines exist for older patients.

There has been some lobbying to more proportionately include older adults in clinical trials, but there is little headway on this front. So we will share what we have learned in our own work experiences as well as from the other Care Managers interviewed about accompanying older adults on their visits to the doctor. And what we have learned about asking questions and doing the extra research on treatments, tests and prescriptions.

6. *Grandma is a Diagnosis.*

Your older loved one is not just a medical condition or a diagnostic label, and they do not have an expiration date either. It is really tempting for a caregiver to fall into the trap of treating an older loved one as if they were a diagnosis such as Alzheimer's disease, congestive heart failure, COPD or some other clinical label. But that narrow labeling misses an important point.

> *Medical care needs to be more thoughtful than a diagnosis and a prescription.*

Most older adults will have multiple concurrent medical conditions, what medical providers refer to as comorbidities. They may have a diagnosis that also makes home a bit more challenging to navigate safely, which now brings into play how to adapt home or make a move. It also is important to think of any diagnosis the same way we all have been encouraged to look at a physical incapacity in a person as something that means they are differently enabled...not disabled as a label. It also plays to what care management is all about: quality of life. The medical model which offers diagnoses followed by prescriptions is narrow and can overlook the psychological, social, physical and spiritual elements of a person's life that together create their quality of life...or lack of quality of life. This book is about what can be learned from other people's experiences that will help the caregiver to preserve as much of what defines a person as possible after their life crisis.

7. *One size fits all.*

Okay, so this has got to be one that everyone already knows. If not, take note of that thing they call a "gown" the next time you visit a hospital as an inpatient yourself. One size rarely fits all. There are books out there that purport to offer you all the tools you will need to care for your aging loved one. Okay, that may be helpful, but you, the caregiver, need to know how the tools apply to your older loved one's very specific predicament.

> ***...for the same reason that everyone's experience with a life crisis or illness or pain is uniquely their own.***

To that end, we are going to offer case studies straight from the Care Managers who have helped to guide caregivers and their care receivers through their crises. In our analyses of case study crises in which Care Managers have been involved, we asked how common these particular situations had been and then for a drill down into examples case by case. By the time we are done, you, too, will begin to see the patterns that Care Managers see in their day to day work.

What we share in the chapters that follow are how specific tools can be applied to the family situations that caregivers are most likely to face. The questions one should ask on behalf of an older loved one clearly will be different if that loved one's diagnosis is dementia versus congestive heart failure. And don't forget there also are over a hundred different kinds of dementia. So, what will be appropriate for Alzheimer's disease may not be appropriate for Lewy Body Disease or vascular dementia, let alone delirium. We will walk you through the lessons learned across hundreds of cases as well as resources that are available in communities and on-line to lend support to families going through crises or just experiencing what we refer to as an ecosystem of aging. We use the term ecosystem, because in any ecosystem what happens to one part within the system/family network affects other parts within the system/family. When dad falls and breaks a hip, it will have an effect on dad, dad's spouse, the adult children, the grandchildren and more. And when a caregiver graduates from being "just stressed" to being totally overwhelmed, it affects the siblings and the care receiver and the care receiver's spouse or partner.

8. *Your care receiver is your priority*.

No! This sounds noble, but it too is a trap. You, the caregiver, are your priority. Actually, it's complicated. There is no doubt that a caregiver is in the role of caring for the older loved one at least in part because that care receiver is important to them. I say "in part" because too often guilt is the primary motivator, and good intentions fall to second or third place, and good judgment falls further back. Caregivers can be the loving and caring people that we all would want to be our "go to" people for our kids, our parents, ourselves. Yet, some of the seemingly best caregivers fail in one of the key survival skills of caregiving; they fail to adequately care for themselves.

> *As a caregiver, you can only take care of another if you are caring also for yourself.*

Listen closely on your next commercial flight when the flight attendant explains that you are to be sure you have your own oxygen mask in place before you attend to a family member with theirs. They know that if you cannot breathe, then there is not much chance you can help anyone else get to the oxygen. At the end of the day, you still need to have enough of you left

34

to fulfill the rest of your responsibilities: being a parent, spouse, friend, employee, and taking care of you!

Chapter Three:

Taking care of the caregiver

Only if you take care of yourself really well can you be the person you need to be for an older loved one. Self-care will be one of the tools we talk about a lot in the chapters that follow. To offer you the most comprehensive perspective on what a caregiver should be anticipating, we asked the dozens of Care Managers we interviewed in 2016 and 2017 to talk to us about their clients. Their experiences with families going through crises of caregiving fall into the following categories:

TYPE OF CASE	%
Alzheimer's Disease,	66.2
Home Safety	66.2
Medication	58.2
Acute Medical Crises	50.3
Inadequate Self-Care	48.0
Chronic Medical	46.8

Family Support	45.5
Residential Transition	39.9
Patient Discharge,	38.6
Financial Challenges	33.7
Other	34.5

What is the important takeaway from this table? It's the numbers. We asked the Care Managers whom we interviewed to tell us what percentages of their clients fall into each of the categories you see.

> *To say that caring for an older loved one is*
> *simple is like saying all it takes*
> *for your car to run is gas.*

It may be no surprise that clients may have more than one issue going on at a time, but the sum total of what you see here is well over 500%! Picture the client who seeks the help of a care manager. The older parent of this family is diagnosed with Alzheimer's disease, but in all likelihood this person also is at risk for what professionals term elopement, or wandering. The care receiver may just wander off, and not recognize where they end up. Hopefully they will be fortunate and be found by a well-intentioned neighbor or police officer who can help them return to the safety of home. So, right off the bat we have dementia and home safety issues, but they also may not be compliant with their medications for a chronic cardiac or respiratory condition. They may have been victimized by a telemarketer to whom they have given their credit card information which is how the family identified that dad has memory issues in the first place. And now the family reaches out for help to find a secure residential option. So, it rarely is just one issue that creates a crisis for the new caregiver; it's a five alarm fire.

Okay, we share this brief example not to scare you to death, but rather to get your attention and let you know what the caregiver reality is all about. This volume is about dementia even though there likely will be more that a care receiver's dementia that needs to be addressed. We include the other major issues highlighted in this table in other volumes, and many of them also are complicated by the other issues that are going on at the same time. Practically speaking the caregivers to an older adult in crisis are faced with a core issue. The example here is about dementia. (We use "dementia" here as an umbrella terms for a family of conditions that can affect cognitive function and memory.) Once the family begins to address the dementia, the other issues will emerge and also need be addressed as well for the ultimate solution to be effective. Likewise, the patient who is being discharged home, but cannot take full care of themselves, may be more about home safety than the illness or accident that originally hospitalized them. Home is where the fall took place that resulted in the fractured hip, hospitalization and rehabilitation. Pending discharge, home may also be less safe if there is no one there to assist in getting about and there may be no food to sustain them through their recovery. There may be a residential change in their future, or perhaps simply a modification of home to make it safer: better lighting for dark hallways, grab bars for the bathroom, clutter cleared, scatter rugs cleared from surfaces and more.

> *Discharge from the hospital is not the end of a "medical care event;" it is the beginning of recovery of quality of life.*

Chapter Four:
Lessons from 350 Care Manager Case Studies

In the interviews with dozens of Care Managers that serve as a foundation for this book, we asked them to take us on "grand rounds." For those of you outside of the jargon that is health care these days, grand rounds is a teaching tool in medical education that exposes new practitioners to what it is that has brought a patient to the hospital, what interventions are being applied, patient progress, prognosis and more.

> **Case studies provide the learning that on the job training does; it is not a textbook.**

These usually are bedside in a hospital, but if you ask any doctor to "work up" a patient like what would be done on grand rounds they know exactly what you want to hear. In our case, we applied this tool in our interviews with Care Managers. We asked them to tell us about older individuals with whom they have worked, diving into the presenting medical conditions or home predicaments, their family or domestic support system, their caregiver(s) and more. We wanted to know outcomes and what a care manager had done to effect a change for the better following the family's crisis.

The results provided the grist for our discussions and recommendations on the pages that follow. The professional Care Managers were very candid in describing what worked and what also did not work quite as they had hoped and even what they might have done differently with the benefit of hindsight. We asked them to rate how challenging each case was and why. As you review some of these cases that we box out in the following chapters appreciate that if a trained care manager says the case had been a "10," that it may have been a "20" to the caregiver family member without the benefit of knowing what help can be brought to bear or what dementia means when they are trying to communicate with mom or dad or simply where to turn for help. We also hope that the case studies bring what otherwise might be just a "caregiver cookbook" closer to a personal sharing that conveys not just what a caregiver's options may be, but what it feels like to be that caregiver in that circumstance. We hope that you will "get" the feelings communicated by these Care Managers, and that you may also hear the stressed caregiver's voice coming through the story.

In the first paragraph we talked about the roller coaster that caregiving can be, so when we asked our Care Managers to rate the challenges of a particular case they may be reflecting on the final resolution to a chaotic ride. Remember roller coasters do not start nor do they end scaring you half to death, but along the way some of the twists, turns and free falls can be absolutely terrifying. As you read further, please appreciate that we thought long and hard about an appropriate title. We hope that the stories we will weave together across the tapestry of caregiving crises will also offer you the lifeline that having a companion along for your ride promises.

As you read the chapters ahead and begin to process the lessons learned from the cases we share, you will find that creating opportunities for success and taking the stress out of caregiving are about following a path and about problem-solving. Yes, there are tools in our toolbox, but the successful cases are more like recipes for a better ending to the crisis. So, while we titled this book the *Caregiver's Coping Companion*, we could just as easily have called it the *Caregiver's Cookbook*. The recipes in this particular Cookbook are far from standard, and they may need a little more of this or a little less of that family crisis by family crisis. As you read you may also come to understand why we call the company we manage Creative Care Management.

PART TWO:

Dementia

> *"You know or suspect that someone close to you has a dementing illness. Where do you go from here? You will need to take stock of your current situation and then identify what needs to be done to help the impaired person and to make the burdens on yourself bearable."*
>
> *~Nancy Mace and Dr. Peter Rabins*
>
> ***The 36-Hour Day***

Chapter Five:

What we know about dementia

Count slowly from one to sixty-seven...one thousand one, one thousand two, one thousand three...by the time you reach one thousand sixty-seven, one more person in the United States will have been diagnosed with Alzheimer's disease. In fact, one in three Americans will die <u>with</u> Alzheimer's disease.

> *Every 67 seconds someone in the United States is diagnosed with Alzheimer's disease.*

There have been new diagnostic breakthroughs and some pharmacological, nutritional and other ways that have proposed to help slow the progression of this disease, but the fact is that they have no substantial or durable effect. Alzheimer's remains the only disease in the top ten causes of death in the United States that cannot be prevented, cured or slowed. And that is just one type of dementia, a label which manifests itself with a number of different names including, but not limited to, Lewy bodies Dementia, vascular dementia, Parkinson's disease, Huntington's disease, mixed dementia and a number of others.

If you talk with anyone of an age these days, you might not be so surprised that most fear a dementia diagnosis more than they fear death itself. So much so that we seem to see the prospect of dementia lurking around most every corner. But just because you forget where you placed your car keys or why you walked into a room and then promptly forgot why you were there does not necessarily mean you are developing some form of dementia. When you forget what the keys are for or when you do not recognize the room you are in, that may be a different story. The fact is that all individuals will have some memory lapses; it is a product of living in this century with multi-tasking and multiple media and multiple people calling for our attention at every turn. In fact, one neurologist calls this manifestation the "dementia of distraction."

> *To say dementia is just forgetfulness is like saying dinner at a pizzeria is just like traveling to Italy.*

And if you don't quite buy that, just walk down any city street and count how many people have their phones in front of them as they navigate the sidewalks. And they talk about distracted driving.

But seriously, any of the clinical dementias that one sees manifest themselves in some sort of impairment of cognitive

48

abilities or compromise of executive function. When mom or dad begin to have difficulty following the instructions of a recipe, or balancing a checkbook or navigating a route to a familiar destination, or returning from the restroom to their table in a crowded restaurant, those may be signs that something is awry. When what used to come easily now results in errors or just plain confusion, it may be time for professional consultation. Some dementias show themselves in changes of mood or increased agitation or a change in how they walk or an increasing withdrawal from the social activities that had in the past been important parts of their lives. One thing that one learns early on is that how a dementia shows itself is almost unique to every individual. This last point is one that you will see in the case studies we will share in this chapter. Dementia is personal. The other major point is that you cannot make the individual with dementia adjust to you and what you want; you must adjust to them and what they now bring once dementia is part of their personality.

Chapter Six:

Dementia, distraction, delirium and depression

Dementia is a category that includes about 100 specific cognitive conditions. Generally speaking, most dementias are diagnoses of exclusion.

> **Not only are there about 100 different types of dementia, but each person's experience with dementia will be as unique as their personalities.**

That is medical talk for the fact that one narrows down what a person is manifesting by successive steps of eliminating other possible explanations for a behavior. For instance, a medical work-up when dementia is suspected will include a review of all the medications a patient may be taking. Some medications have a pronounced effect on a person's memory.

Benadryl (generically known as diphenhydramine) was first approved by the FDA years ago to help with the sinus issues of seasonal or other allergies, and it still is used in that capacity. But the active ingredient is also used in a host of sleep aids, because the pronounced side effect, drowsiness, can be a desirable main effect for those having difficulty sleeping through the night. Unfortunately, there is yet another side effect; it also can impair memory when used long term. Some other medications, when a person is not compliant, can impair memory or impart some amount of confusion. People who are prescribed levothyroxine, for instance, for their hypothyroidism may appear confused or disoriented if they do not adhere to their regimen and their hormones are not well-controlled (i.e., if their thyroid stimulating hormone levels run high).

Against all of the potential warning signs for possible dementia, be careful about a hasty judgment. A change in mental acuity that is rapid in its onset is better classified as a delirium – not dementia. These episodes can arise from urinary tract or other infections, dehydration or even some hormonal imbalances. Certain medications like steroids or combinations of medications can precipitate short term cognitive imbalances.

> ***Delirium* differs from *dementia* in that it has a rapid onset and it typically also will be transient.**

Caregivers should be alert to these, but not jump to the wrong conclusions.

And beware of your loved one's healthcare provider who prescribes any of the Alzheimer's agents for "organic dementia" or "delirium" or anything short of a definitive Alzheimer's disease diagnosis. A prescription against a false diagnosis will do no good, and may even be harmful.

False Alarms for Dementia.

If your loved one is of a certain age it is common that there will be keys misplaced or names forgotten and more. Yet, that is not necessarily an indication of anything organically wrong with your loved one's memory. So, how does one know? Here are some warning signs according to the medical experts:

- Neurologists talk about the differences between "retrieval" and "storage" problems in memory. Forgetting someone's name is retrieval and it is not a warning sign of Alzheimer's. Forgetting that you know the person at all, however, is a storage problem, and it can be a sign of a more serious brain issue. Or misplacing the keys is a retrieval issue, but forgetting what the keys are supposed to do is a storage problem that should prompt closer attention.

- There also is a difference between losing the car keys and losing the ability to do something that always has come naturally. Misplacing the keys, according to the experts, can happen to just about anyone, but forgetting how to start the car and put it in gear should be cause for concern. Or the loved one who was always good at math forgetting how to multiply also may be concerning.

- Just plain confusion with normal daily activities also is a potential sign, according to the scientists who study these things. If your loved one gets confused on the way back to your table from the restroom while dining out, that may be cause for concern. You should also look for smaller signs as basic as their stride. If their steps begin to more resemble a shuffle this may be a sign of a more fundamental uncertainty...or the unexplained fall likewise can be a precursor of cognitive decline.

- Finally, look for what may be as subtle as small changes in personality. The loved one who used to be the animated conversationalist, but who now is more subdued may be responding to their own confusion in trying to follow what everyone is saying. Agitation or a short temper in a person who was once a cheery individual also can be a sign of changing mental abilities.

Consider when your loved one last had a complete physical. By complete, we mean one in which all the medications they may have been taking are reconsidered. This is especially true if your loved one sees multiple providers each prescribing against the conditions in which they specialize; what the cardiologist prescribes may not "mix" well with what the neurologist or pulmonologist are prescribing. There may also be subtle cues

54

that some have missed without a thorough exam that could include a neuropsychiatric evaluation or even something as basic as a hearing test.

Research reported at the 2016 Alzheimer's Association International Conference highlights some early findings on sensory changes that may be better leading indicators than even MRIs of cognitive decline. One study pointed to impaired odor identification as a leading indicator of cognitive impairment, and another pointed to thinning of the retinal nerve fiber as a predictor of failing cognitive function. Such research efforts are preliminary and probably not anything that can yet be applied by families of potential sufferers, but they offer the promise of useful information that may one day be something that families can use as an early warning of trouble on the horizon.

Chapter Seven:

Prevention, diagnostics, treatments, resources, support

In 2011 revised guidelines for diagnosing Alzheimer's were introduced and one of the big steps was a recognition that the disease really is present before cognitive symptoms show themselves. Because Alzheimer's is about the nerve damage in the brain, a cornerstone of medical diagnosis is the imaging of the beta amyloid plaque (protein fragments) that is deposited in the brain along with the twisted brain tangles that signify nerve cell death and brain damage.

> *Alzheimer's may be <u>suspected</u> by your older loved one's primary care physician, but it can be <u>diagnosed</u> only through neuro-psych testing and sophisticated imaging.*

These are assessed by brain imaging – using magnetic resonance imaging (MRI) or computerized tomography (CT) scanning – and may be present long before any cognitive impairment is manifested. The proteins also leave their trail in cerebrospinal fluid which can be detected in lab tests. A couple decades ago these tells were only discovered by autopsy after an Alzheimer's patient had died. As the disease progresses, there will be cognitive impairment that becomes the signature of Alzheimer's disease, and this is determined through fairly rigorous mental testing in a neuro-psychological medical work-up.

Vascular dementia is a distinct condition with its origin in ruptures and bleeding in the vessels that feed the brain, sometimes through mini-strokes or transient ischemic attacks (TIAs). Imaging of the brain will show the telltale signs of these blood vessel blockages or problems, and cognitive testing will tell the rest of the story. And the list goes on as one sorts through the rest of the players in what is a very populated category of dementia manifestations.

Who is at risk for dementia?

The simple answer is that in only about one in twenty cases is there any leading indicator or marker for Alzheimer's in the form of a specific gene, and these are the early onset (before middle age) cases.   There also is the ApoE4 gene variant. Individuals with one copy of this variant can have as much as four times the risk as others in developing the disease, and two copies of ApoE4 increase the risk to tenfold. Women also are at somewhat greater risk than men. And sadly, not only are women more likely to be diagnosed with the disease, but they also are more likely to be a caregiver to someone with the disease.   For all other cases, it is simply a matter of increasing risk as one ages.

> *Scientists are just beginning to identify genetic markers or other precursors of Alzheimer's disease.*

The risk factors in general across all the dementias tend to revolve around birthdays, poor diet, poor exercise, poor intellectual/ social engagement as well as diabetes, high blood pressure or depression.   For the dementias that are specific to either Parkinson's or Huntington's, the cognitive compromises simply accompany the physical progressions of these diseases.

The processed food consumption that has been linked to our global epidemic of obesity is also tied to the rising rates of Alzheimer's disease world-wide.   We don't mean to sound the alarm about sugar, but we came across an article recently that tied together a number of facts and trends that we all may have seen. And we all should be very alarmed!

As professional care managers, we often work with older adults who have developed medical conditions that reflect a lifetime of poor health and nutrition habits. We see the elevated blood pressure and the obesity that can arise from sedentary lifestyles and poor diet. One of the more common developments we see is the onset of type-2 diabetes resulting from a lifetime of too many sweets, poor diet in general and lack of exercise that have resulted in what doctors call "insulin resistance," the pancreas' inability to keep producing enough insulin to process all the carbohydrates or sugar.

What you may not know is that the brain also produces insulin, and that when faced with a prolonged assault from more sugar than it can process, its ability to produce insulin may falter and then fail.

> **The brain can suffer from sugar overload in many of the ways the pancreas does in diabetics.**

The result is referred to as "type-3 diabetes." The research has been piling up. For instance, people who suffer from type-2 diabetes (type-1 is the form that people are either born with or develop as an immune response) have deposits of amyloid-beta in their pancreas. Sound familiar? Yes, amyloid beta deposits in the brain are a signature marker for Alzheimer's disease. And this also begins to explain why type-2 diabetics are estimated to be anywhere from 50 percent to 100 percent more likely than others to also develop insulin-resistant Alzheimer's disease.

Type-2 diabetes does not cause Alzheimer's disease, but type-3 diabetes is caused by the same poor diet that causes type-2 diabetes. This may begin to also explain why the rates of the two conditions both have tripled in the United States in the past forty years. This, along with a lot of other inflammatory conditions related to the heart and the circulatory system. In related research scientists have found that one of the more common medications used to treat type 2 diabetes, metformin, has a neuroprotective benefit as well as its indicated benefit in addressing blood sugar levels and pancreatic function. The research coming out of a close analysis of Veterans Administration data by a doctoral candidate at Tulane University suggests that metformin can have a long term neuroprotective effect that can stave off the brain deterioration of Alzheimer's and Parkinson's.

The extra care required for the estimated 5.4 million obese Americans with type-2 diabetes is costing us a lot - $150 billion annually! But hold on. It is estimated that care for that many Alzheimer's patients is going to be even higher at about $200 billion a year, the reason being, in part, because the close supervision for the safety of a cognitively-impaired patient is so much higher than for an obese individual.

This is probably one of the situations where we don't have to connect the dots for any of you who are caregivers to an older adult...or attending even to your own well-being.

> *The combined effect of the obesity epidemic and the dementia epidemic will be a caregiver crisis of need outstripping supply.*

Our advice can best be summed up with two words: diet, exercise. Ironically, these are considered first line treatment for people who are obese or who have begun showing the signs of type-2 diabetes or elevated blood pressure on a number of other chronic, inflammatory conditions.

Are there any medications for preventing/stopping dementia?

The science is still fairly thin on most fronts, but there is increasing opportunity to find effective treatments as science begins to peel back the layers of this complicated set of diseases and their complex etiologies. There is some evidence to encourage taking vitamin D to help stave off dementia, but it is not the rigorous sort of clinical evidence that offers much more than a promise presently. Some tout the virtues of gingko biloba as a memory booster, but there is no evidence that it works on dementia. Others recommend "clean diets" that center on organic or non-GMO foods, but again, there is no rigorous, scientific evidence to support the claims.

Until very recently, most research has found little support for the benefits of nutritional supplements or nutraceuticals in either preventing or slowing the progression of neurodegenerative diseases.

> **While there is no cure for neurodegenerative disease yet, there is promising research on vitamins and nutrition.**

But Jennifer Lemon, Ph.D., a research associate in the Department of Medical Physics and Applied Radiation Sciences at McMaster University in Canada, conducted controlled studies using laboratory mice that show real promise. (Note that animal studies, such as those using mice, are almost always the first step toward research that will move to human subjects later, and virtually all mammal brain functions are similar metabolically.) Dr. Lemon gave a mix of vitamins and minerals, along with nutraceuticals, such as beta carotene, bioflavonoids, cod liver oil, flax seed, garlic, and green tea extract to one group of mice. Relative to another group of mice receiving no nutraceuticals, the treated mice maintained better brain cell numbers and mass and cognitive function. The treated mice seemed also to preserve their sight and sense of smell, two capabilities associated with neurodegenerative decline. Much research remains to be done, but we ought not be too hasty in giving up on the supplements you can purchase at the corner health food store.

At this writing, FDA has approved five drugs to treat - not cure - Alzheimer's:

- <u>Aricept</u> (donepezil) is able to claim that it can slow the cognitive progression of Alzheimer's and modestly improve confusion, memory and awareness.
- <u>Exelon</u> (rivastigmine) claims to address the memory loss of both Parkinson's and Alzheimer's.
- <u>Namenda</u> (memantine) claims to treat the moderate to severe confusion of Alzheimer's disease, but it is to be used in combination with one of the other agents.
- <u>Namzaric</u> (donepezil and memantine) combines an extended release form of Namenda as well as Aricept in one pill to address the symptoms each addresses individually.
- <u>Razadyne</u> (galantamine) claims to improve the ability to think and even remember by increasing brain levels of acetylcholine, a beneficial enzyme.

More information can be found at www.webmd.com/search.

At the risk of over-generalizing, all of these medications either slow the breakdown of the helpful enzyme acetylcholine or slow/stop the production of either glutamate or acetylcholinesterase in the brain. None of them has a great impact on the diseases they are to address, and none works for long.

All of this is just the beginning. If you look to the level of clinical activity in the area of Alzheimer's treatments, it begins to tell the story.

> *While there are only modestly effective pharmaceutical interventions for dementia now, there are thousands of clinical trials investigating new therapies.*

As of this writing a federal web site that is the repository for all sanctioned clinical research into treatments for just Alzheimer's shows 3,065 studies into treatments or cures for one form of dementia or another.

The same site shows 1,780 studies in progress specifically for Alzheimer's disease. Some of these studies are focused on the dementias after they have been diagnosed and unfortunately brain damage has occurred. Others look farther "upstream" in the hope of finding out how to stop these progressive diseases before they begin to take root. There is much to be excited about. Some of these studies are still recruiting individuals who may wish to participate in a clinical trial, not just in the hope of receiving a medicine that may stave off their disease's progression, but in the hope that their participation will advance the cause for the next family that is visited by their crisis. www.clinicaltrials.gov

Preventing dementia?

Many researchers have been trying to figure this out. So far there are few clear answers, but the emerging data on the VA data as well as the Canadian research among nutraceuticals are

65

promising. There also are hints that behaviors that keep us healthy and engaged — exercise, healthy diet, social activities, educational activities — may help hold dementia at bay, probably because those behaviors promote overall brain and body health, as well as emotional well-being. Education may promote what is called cognitive reserve, essentially the idea that the more we learn and therefore stimulate our brains, the more brain cells we have that can temporarily compensate for some memory and thinking problems. But no vitamin, supplement or brain game has been found to be a magic wand.

There may be steps that a middle aged individual can take that will quantifiably reduce their risks of dementia, at least according to long term research recently released from the University of Eastern Finland. Very simply, what the Finnish researchers set out to do was study what kind of influence healthy diet could have among individuals from midlife as they aged. The researchers developed an index which helped them to quantify what constituted a "healthy diet" versus what they considered to be an "unhealthy diet." Healthy foods included unsaturated fats from milk products as well as fish, fruits, berries and vegetables. Unhealthy foods, on the other hand, included saturated fats, salty fish, sweetened drinks, other sweets, eggs and sausages.

> *Maybe they were right in the seventies:*
> *we are what we eat.*

At the end of fourteen years, those who had eaten the healthiest foods had a 90% lower risk of developing dementia than those whose diets were the least healthy. These individuals started the program at about fifty years of age and the final assessment was in their mid-sixties. Those participants who had the highest consumption of saturated fats at the outset of the study were at higher risk of being diagnosed with "mild cognitive impairment" at the 21 year point in the study as well. This link between saturated fat consumption and incidence of cognitive impairment was consistent among the panel of participants. But there was another finding about coffee that may come as something of a surprise. They found that the "sweet spot" was three to five cups of coffee a day. That is to say the researchers found that those who consumed fewer than three as well as those who consumed more than five cups of coffee a day had higher risks for developing dementia over the courses of their lives. Something of a "happy medium."

What should people in their middle years make of this study? The researchers had used this measure of a healthy diet based on the sum total of what a person consumes because they argued that there are a lot of interactions across foods and nutrients. That said, it also makes it difficult to point to a single food that is the miracle "dementia stopper." In reality, maybe it is just that...well, that there is no one food that is going to make us healthier or one that will make us inherently less healthy. If you want to make it to your later years without as great a fear

67

of cognitive decline, should you eat less saturated fats and consume more fruits, berries and vegetables along with an average – 3 to 5 cups - dose of coffee. These researchers would probably say that it couldn't hurt.

There is also some noteworthy prospective work at the Alzheimer's Prevention Clinic at Weill Cornell Medicine and New York Presbyterian Hospital. For about three years now they have been tracking individuals who have not started with any cognitive or memory issues. That may sound odd if they are looking to identify what works in treating a memory condition like Alzheimer's but it really goes to the heart of the issue. No one begins with Alzheimer's disease. It only emerges slowly from very subtle changes into increasingly dramatic deficits that eventually take away everything but the present.

The Alzheimer's Prevention Clinic sees patients who initially are not at all symptomatic, and they interview them, record a rigorous family and medical history and get very granular with the information. Like the Finnish researchers, they are looking for what may become leading indicators or risk factors and markers, but they also are looking for something more. They are looking for ways to begin to categorize all these patients according to risk factors that can be quantified. They are using a range of computer-assisted and traditional pencil and paper cognitive tests to grade the patients. From all of these they tailor a personal regimen using what nutritional, behavioral and physical programs are thought to offer some benefit. They then continue to chart everyone's progress, and they will continue with this over the long run.

They are looking for changes in key biomarkers, beta amyloid levels in the brain and blood glucose and glucose metabolic levels in the brain. What they identify as departures from the norm or from what is calibrated as healthy, they will carefully examine to see what may have precipitated these turns. You can imagine that it would be great to link such efforts with the research that shows protein tau to be a more sensitive early warning sign of dementia than even beta amyloid. And what has yielded positive outcomes as well. It is the goal of this program to evolve new, personalized health plans that can help future patients toward even better outcomes. Consider it to be a disease prevention program that succeeds by closing off all the access points through which the disease invades healthy bodies.

While we await the results of some of these ongoing research efforts, it is important to note that dementia is not inevitable, and there are steps we all can take - at any age - to stave off cognitive decline.

> *Consume Omega-3 fatty acids, sleep well, avoid distractions and avoid sleep aids or night-time alcohol.*

Here are five.

- **Go fish** - You probably have heard or read that fish oil is healthy for your brain, and a number of studies have supported that notion. The antioxidative omega-3 fatty acids in fish oil seem to be an aid to later life brain health. Researchers have quantified this beneficial effect in clinical studies comparing people who consume omega-3 with those who do not. Eat fish.

  Sound sleep - The estimates of sleep apnea's prevalence range from 25 to 40+ million adults in the United States alone. The most common and obvious product of this nightly disturbance of sleep is the excessive daytime sleepiness that results, a sleepiness that over time not only reduces quality of life, but if unchecked, it also impairs memory as well as general motor coordination, ability to concentrate and a number of other facets of cognitive function. So if you know someone who has sleep apnea, get help. Sleep well.

- **Sleep aids** - A good night's sleep is precious, but using a prescription sleep aid may be a mixed blessing. There is evidence that some of the prescription solutions for sleeplessness cause selective amnesia or even hallucinations or sleep activity. People on some of these agents have reportedly engaged in sleep driving, making telephone calls or even preparing and eating food with no recall of the events. The cure for sleeplessness may be worse than the condition. Sleep healthy.

- **Night caps** - It is true that alcohol can make one drowsy, but it does not enhance the quality of sleep. Researchers have shown that alcohol disrupts the formation of memories in the brain. It may not be dementia, strictly speaking, but recurring memory lapses can make day to day functioning a bit shaky. Sleep clean.

- **Single Tasking** - Multi-tasking may be the hallmark of the 21st century, but far from making us more productive, it actually hinders cognitive productivity. One researcher refers to this as the: "dementia of distraction," the kind where you walk into a room while checking your phone for a text, but then forget why you entered the room. This dementia knows no age requirements, because teenagers can be as prone to the distraction of multi-tasking as older adults. Task singly.

As you may imagine, the list could actually go on and on, but the dos and don'ts of this short review highlight what to embrace and what to avoid in order to enhance cognitive function at almost any age. What is the first thing you learn when you are admitted to a hospital, and this can be for outpatient or inpatient procedures? ONE SIZE DOES NOT FIT ALL!

That applies to Alzheimer's disease as well. There has been no blockbuster fix for Alzheimer's, to date, but on closer examination of how people with different genes or with different make-ups respond, scientists are finding they react differently to medications. We already have seen this in cancer treatment, and it is a broad and promising side of medical care called genomics...sometimes called pharmacogenomics when referring to medicines and nutrigenomics for foods or supplements. When physicians look to a person's specific genes, they can find people who may respond a lot better than someone without those genes. They call it "personalized medicine," and it is showing some real promise.

Let's start with a clinical failure that may actually be something else altogether: tramiprosate (an antiaggregation of amyloid agent). Earlier this year results from a phase 3 clinical trial (this is the final phase for a drug to be up for possible approval by FDA) for tramiprosate showed no appreciable improvement, on average, for Alzheimer's subjects in the trial versus those on placebo. I said, "On average." When scientists later looked more closely at the genetic makeup of patients in the trial, they found that those patients with two copies of the APOE4-gene had markedly better results than those with only one or no copies of this gene. Scientists are reassessing how these patients and those with the APOE3 gene respond, especially since these latter are at greater risk for developing Alzheimer's disease. Worth a second look, for sure.

I also mentioned nutraceuticals. In a European study some time ago, there seemed to be some promise for vitamin D as a protective agent against Alzheimer's. As scientists looked specifically at the patients with two copies of the APOE4 gene and taking vitamin D, they found those patients had better memory scores than those on placebo or without the gene. Vitamin D in the absence of the two gene copies did not seem to do as well.

Scientists are also looking more closely at omega-3, what we sometimes refer to as fish oil (it is only in the fish oil, because that is where it is stored after fish eat the algae that contain the omega-3). And there are multiple types of omega-3, two of which are particularly "brain-healthy." Scientists have a couple challenges here. One, the brain's absorption of the healthy omega-3 takes a few years, and there also is a difference in the genes I mentioned above. This may take longer to get good evidence, but it also is promising.

There also is research into limiting environmental risk for developing Alzheimer's that is linked to both the APOE4 gene and the presence of pesticides like DDT and its metabolic cousin, DDE. While DDT has been banned in America for some time, its metabolite, DDE, is still around. Preliminary research suggests that it is not just the DDE or just the APOE4 gene, but the presence of both that is associated with higher incidence of Alzheimer's.

While these early findings will not tell you what to ask your physician about diet or medications, it is a cautionary note for all who live in or near agricultural regions. The lesson learned again is that we likely have just begun to tap the genotypic profiles that may lend themselves to less versus more risk or less versus more success. The oncology field has begun to get better and better results in their fights across a number of cancer types by paying attention to genes that can predispose individuals to either greater risks or to better outcomes. It just may be that Alzheimer's disease can follow the same model.

Talking to Dementia.

If you are a caregiver to someone with dementia you may have found that communication can be frustrating, but you need to remember how frustrating communication is for your loved one. It is important right off the top to appreciate that the dementia patient is going to be frustrated as they try to address not just your questions, but perhaps even who you are.

> *Talking to a loved one with dementia can be frustrating for you, but remember how much <u>more frustrating</u> it is for the person with the dementia.*

This confusion can manifest itself as anxiety (imagine being perpetually lost), irritability, poor self-esteem or depression (but only if they are aware of their condition). Appreciate also that most forms of dementia are progressive medical conditions that will worsen over time requiring you to adapt your communication to meet their changing needs.

The memory loss is the proverbial tip of the iceberg as a dementia sufferer is grappling not with just forgetfulness, but also disorientation, confusion, word finding and fear. A caregiver needs to be able to put aside the loss that they feel as they approach someone in the throes of a mind-robbing condition. The dementia care receiver is the limiting factor on what kinds of communication can be expected. And their dementia will be complicated by simple co-morbidities such as vision or hearing loss. If the patient cannot hear all that is said or everyone who is speaking, or if they cannot pick up on the subtle visual cues that are part of "normal" conversation, it will amplify what is dementia. And don't forget to factor in the anxiety or frustration the patient may also feel as a consequence of any of these deficits. Talk to them based on where they are coming from by keeping in the moment and accommodating all that they must accommodate.

Follow these tips for more effective communication for you both:

- When you first approach the dementia sufferer, do it from the front so as not to startle them; if they are not family, use their formal name – Mr. Jones – as you address them and maintain eye contact.
- Be calm and reassuring by speaking slowly and in a gentle tone, using simple words; repeat yourself if

necessary or rephrase only after trying the same wording a couple times.

- Take your time speaking so that the patient can take their time to process your question and formulate a response; and remember to pose just one question at a time.

Do not disagree; gently redirect. If your loved one speaks of meeting their spouse whom you know died several years ago, gently change the subject or even ask about what plans they may have. If you insist that the spouse has died they will only experience the shock of the loss anew.

> **It is no longer about who is right or wrong;**
> **it is about the one who cannot remember.**

- How you speak and how you look will be as important as what you are saying, so smile and speak in a gentle voice.
- Humor can be relaxing to both you and the dementia sufferer, but always be careful to not make them feel they are the object of the humor.
- If the dementia sufferer is a loved one, hugs and touches are every bit as important now as they may have been when the patient was more lucid.
- Try to keep to a regular schedule of daily activities with a dementia patient to help them feel the comfort of a

routine; change is difficult and can create unnecessary anxiety.

- Appreciate that early learning may stay for a long time after the dementia sufferer no longer tracks a given conversation; in religious services we have found that an individual may not track a new reading, but they can recite an old familiar one.

- While a dementia patient may take longer to dress themselves, it is important to allow them to do so. If you begin doing tasks for them, they may lose the ability to take care of themselves entirely.

Chapter Eight:

Eight Lessons Learned from 70 Care Manager Case Studies

The case studies that are the focus of this chapter are really all about how families are addressing dementia when it gets personal. Alzheimer's is one of those crises that does not make an appointment. What can a caregiver learn from others about how to cope with a loved one whose mind is disappearing before them?

> *Your loved one with dementia probably feels more alone than you do.*

From our interviews we accumulated **70** case studies in which some form of dementia was central to the challenges of the families involved. We offer eight of these that help to illustrate some important lessons that will benefit all families who are confronted with what arguably is a diagnosis more feared than terminal illness itself. It is an illness that Marilyn Mitchell (author of Dancing on Quicksand: A Gift of Friendship in the Age of Alzheimer's) refers to as a "trauma (that) includes the horror of being separated from one's self, a self-made up largely of one's memories ... Dementia brings new meaning to the word alone."

Each case study should be viewed as a snapshot of a specific point in time in the lives of the caregiver and care receiver. No representation is made to suggest or imply that the events shared here owe entirely to just the dementia.

Case Study 1.1

Lesson Learned: First, diagnose - dementia, delirium, distraction, depression, decompensation

- *Visit the Alzheimer's Association web site for background*
- *Get a clear diagnosis*
- *Find a practitioner who can help set the caregiver's expectations*

(ID: E22) The caregiver is 54 years old and lives next door to her 90 year old mother whose precipitating medical problem was an acute exacerbation of shingles. To add to the mix, the daughter's father was in hospice care at a local facility, a challenge that weighed on both the daughter and the mother and split the daughter's already fragmented time.

Once a care manager was called in, the mother was taken to a new primary care physician, a geriatrician, who prescribed a number of anti-viral medications to help manage and reduce the shingles infection. Once that condition came under better control, she was also diagnosed with early stage Alzheimer's disease. The initial discomfort and agitation associated with the pain of shingles had made an earlier diagnosis challenging. The physician helped to explain to the daughter how her mother's dementia could be best managed. The doctor showed that 80% of the mother's medications were over-the-counter medications which he reduced to one OTC in combination with two other remaining prescription medications.   With prompting, the physician also offered reading materials for the daughter as well as contact information for a local dementia caregiver support group.

Long term, the care manager was asked to make wellness visits on the mom three times a week to be the daughter's "eyes and ears" as well as offer the daughter some respite from the grind of daily support for her mother. Ironically, the daughter's visit schedule was sufficient that the mother felt she was, in fact, enjoying a daily visit from her daughter. At the recommendation of the Care Manager and with a physician's referral, an occupational therapist also was brought in for sessions with the mother to maximize her ability to navigate her home and care for herself as independently as possible.

OUR TAKEAWAY: The family demands for the daughter to be with both her mother and father at the same time and the mother's desire to be with her husband while not understanding his predicament or her dementia created added stressors for the caregiver/daughter as she worked to balance the demands of her own life with those of her aging parents. It is important to note what is NOT part of this case study. Living alone and living with Alzheimer's is potentially dangerous. This case could have been handled more aggressively by bringing in round the clock care; a diagnosis with Alzheimer's is the proverbial "fork in the road" where caregiving vigilance steps up. Moderate to mid-stage dementias like this are "elopements" waiting to happen. Once a patient "wanders," it usually brings in law enforcement which then brings in Adult Protective Services and possibly the courts. Preventing escalation like that should be on the mind of any caregiver to a loved one diagnosed with Alzheimer's. There are multiple risks associated with allowing a dementia patient to prepare their own meals. It is not simply "playing with fire," but there is the risk associated with forgetting to turn off burners or ovens.

Case Study 1.2

Lesson Learned: Help reinforce a calm, predictable environment

- *Reduce background noise and distractions*
- *Give them more time for tasks*
- *Do not argue with their point of view; redirect*

(ID: E51)The caregiver is the 40 year old daughter of a 71 year old woman with diagnosed with early stage Alzheimer's disease. The daughter lives at distance out of state, 2,000 miles away. While the mother is a risk for elopement, or wandering, she is most comfortable staying in her home with her husband of nearly 50 years. They are both first generation immigrants from

India, and their long term marriage, family values and custom weigh heavily in her choices.

A care manager was brought in, and she began by setting the mother up with homemaker services. Initially this was 20 hours a week...the early hours to help her get dressed and showered for the day and again at night to change into her pajamas. There was also some meal preparation from the homemaker. A volunteer was also present twice a week to help her "mall walk." The home was fitted with a personal emergency alert system that included a pendant/button she would wear with her at all times. (These can give a false sense of security as the button is only as good as the person who can remember to press it when needed.) Her husband, whose faculties were intact, was able to "escape to his basement shop" when the caregivers were present.

The long term goal is to maintain the mother safely in her own home, and this is particularly important as she is not fluent in English. Her success in no small part owes to the daughter's compilation of a "mom manual" on how to care for her mother. This predictable regimen adds to the mother's comfort and ease while she cannot recall her daily activities from moment to moment. The mother's comfort also owes to the effective collaboration among all those charged with her care and a full respect for her culturally-specific habits and activities.

OUR TAKEAWAY: This case became the equivalent of couple's therapy with the challenging dynamic revolving around trying to meet both spouses' housing and self-care needs. The homemaker did help with light housekeeping to some extent, but absent from the calculus again is the potential for elopement. That said, in early stages, dementia sufferers are not inclined to leave familiar surroundings...unless part of their past habits includes routine trips to the store, the salon, the fitness center, etc.

Case Study 1.3

Lesson Learned: Communicate where they are.

- *Forgive them when they do not remember your last call*
- *Communicate with them in their reality, their time (listen, acknowledge, redirect)*
- *Do not correct their recall if it will resurrect pain*

(ID: E34) The caregiver is the 55 year old daughter who lives in the same community as her 83 year old mother. Mother has been disoriented and agitated, and has now been in and out of a number inpatient psychiatric facilities. (It is not common that a memory unit will accept someone whose second diagnosis is a psychiatric disorder, particularly if it contributes to aggressive or agitated behavior.) She now is able to stay in an assisted living facility with appropriately-trained staff. This may explain her numerous relocations prior to this. Her other psychiatric issues and the subsequent array of medications had been confounding her self-care. In addition, the staff had not been trained in redirecting her attention when she became agitated. (Agitation is one of the hallmarks of vascular dementia that can help distinguish it from other dementias.)

During an inpatient hospitalization a new psychiatrist was brought in for an evaluation and it was his care plan that began to ween her off some of the five psychiatric medications she had been taking. Once an assisted living facility with a staff trained in dementia care was identified, the combination of a more supportive environment and a reduction in meds reduced some of the agitation. Appreciate that a clear psychiatric diagnosis has been essential.

Over the longer term, the care receiver had been successfully weaned off three of her psychiatric medications, and she has now successfully remained in assisted living and out of the hospital. Clarifying her primary diagnosis as dementia allowed her to be removed from a number of her medications which likely were exacerbating her dementia. The daughter has become the "cheerleader" of the care manager who coordinated the interventions.

OUR TAKEAWAY: The daughter became, in the words of the professional care manager, "one of my biggest cheerleaders." The key was an accurate primary diagnosis. The next steps then revolved around finding an assisted living facility with a staff who understood how to communicate with the mother and encourage her comfort and reinforce her sense of safety.

Case Study 1.4

Lesson Learned: Preserve safety and quality of life.

- *Elopement is a home security risk from the inside out*
- *Dementia is a risk for scams, assault and exposure*
- *Identify what can still be done safely — independently or with help*

(ID: E33) The caregiver is the 59 year old daughter, one of six siblings, who are dispersed around the country. Their father, a widower, is an insulin-dependent diabetic, but in good physical health otherwise. The father manifests some frontal lobe dementia, a condition which increases impulsivity, and which has caused him to lose almost a million dollars on women and gambling, the combination of which has placed him at risk for bankruptcy. Enter the professional care manager into what amounted to a five alarm fire. With a coordinated intervention, the father was placed on a strict budget with his son, a banker, overseeing his bankruptcy proceeding - which is about to be resolved.

While the father is under financial control, he also must be kept in a monitored environment as he is too aggressive with younger women owing to his poor impulse control. He has been successfully moved to assisted living to help mitigate his elopement risk and better manage his blood glucose levels. The father has been "a handful" in the words of the staff, but once trust had been established, he could be cajoled into responding to reasonable demands. His long term prospects are very favorable.

OUR TAKEAWAY: Helping the father get to a facility and to care that could set appropriate boundaries and protect him from exploitation could not have been possible without proper legal paperwork in place. While guardianship may not be a necessary part of a solution in a case like this, having powers of attorney for both healthcare and finance had been key. The professional care manager extolls the virtues of the staff who could gain the care receiver's trust, and soon he was relatively easy to redirect – or as she put it, cajole – him into more socially-appropriate behavior.

Case Study 1.5

Lesson Learned: How to Address the Dementia with Limited Resources.

- *Not everyone has all the funds to "pay their own way"*
- *There are (almost) always options if you ask enough questions*
- *The government continues to be a safety net*

(ID: E71) The only caregiver in this case study is really not in the picture. This 60 year old nephew of a 95 year old widower is at distance geographically and is overwhelmed by the rest of his life responsibilities. The uncle has had a hands-on caregiver for the past three years and has been a widower for two years. The care manager was called in because the uncle was at risk for outlasting his money owing principally to a mistake by his bank in calculating his means and his needs. That, and he now is at the point that his dementia requires full-time care at the same time his ability to ambulate is declining.

Being 95 may have been this individual's silver lining, however, since it also meant that he had served in the military during the Second World War. He was therefore entitled to Veterans' benefits. In this instance, the VA was also able to supply a professional who would visit the gentleman in his home to help with the paperwork and then expedite the processing once the necessary forms were complete. He was also qualified for Medicaid which made it possible to begin a search for a nursing home with a secure memory unit. In our collective experience, starting with Medicaid will exclude some facilities

89

from the list. Many facilities have a policy of accepting Medicaid, but only after the applicant has exhausted private resources. The care manager further reported that all the paperwork for both Medicaid and for the VA was approved within six weeks of submitting the materials.

In the meantime, our gentleman had been able to qualify for a reverse mortgage which afforded some flexibility in shopping about for a facility. He continued to live at home with care brought to him for his safety and well-being.

OUR TAKEAWAY: As THE Care Manager described this case study, she said that the urgency of the situation required a lot of problem-solving and knowing what to do and whom to call. It is not, she claims, that other family members could not have done the same, but it helps to have been down similar paths in the past. To these considerations we would add that Medicaid rules are subject to periodic revisions, and they vary somewhat by state. It is important to stay current.

Case Study 1.6

Lesson Learned: Two People Require Two Solutions.

- *Think of it as couples therapy – the caregiver and the care receiver*

- *The big challenge typically is residential, especially with dementia*
- *Appreciate also that adult children can multiply the issues with their needs*

(ID: E70) The caregiver is the 80 year old husband, and the wife is in her late 70's but has been diagnosed with dementia. It is a role reversal that has been evolving in slow motion as the wife had been caring for her husband owing to his multiple back surgeries with poor outcomes. Over time, her increasing dementia has left her unable to do the normal activities of daily living. She had begun to be increasingly agitated, especially with being unable to navigate cooking in her own home. Because of the escalating needs of the wife – especially the constant monitoring – the home care aides who have been brought in are overwhelmed and the husband is neglected.

The 60 year old daughter sought the help of a care manager to help sort things out. The care manager convened a group meeting with the husband and the adult children to address the core issue: how to get the couple the care they need when they each need quite different care. A new agency with special skills around dementia was recommended, but the long range solution was also provided. That long range solution very simply was assisted living, but living arrangements could require separate residences for the husband and wife. Some facilities will allow the cognitively-intact partner to live with a

91

spouse in a memory unit and be able personally to come and go at will. This depends on the facility's ability to accommodate couples with different cognitive capacities.

The family "gets" that dad is not getting the care he requires, but the husband is the passive member of the couple and is willing to allow his spouse to dictate terms for their collective care. That said, he still must receive the help he needs based on how is activities of daily living, nutritional and social needs.

OUR TAKEAWAY: We and the care manager concur that this situation likely will only be resolved when the family IS confronted with a precipitating crisis. With dementia, it is common that an elopement by the dementia sufferer will catalyze action, especially if Adult Protective Services enters the picture. The other event could involve the husband suffering a fall or other physical injury when he tries to assist his wife or restrain her when she becomes agitated. Vigilance on the part of the home health agency team is paramount, but this ultimately is a waiting game. Most facilities also have clear language regarding the extent to which a resident's personal choice is allowed only insofar as it does not endanger the safety and security of others.

Case Study 1.7

Lesson Learned: When it's tech versus touch.

- *If agency personnel are not acceptable, technology can help*
- *Technology can be eyes and ears for the caregiver*
- *Technology should be complemented by personnel*

(ID: E69) The caregiver is the 60 year old daughter of a mother in her early 90's who has been diagnosed with the early stages of Alzheimer's The mother lives alone and has had some confusion keeping her medication schedules organized. She also shows some signs of self-care issues with inadequate supplies of food and some evidence of mold in the refrigerator. Additionally, her home has a number of areas that are poorly lit which will add to any confusion in the evening hours when she cannot see clearly to navigate.

The daughter has opted for remotely monitored cameras to monitor mom. She has been encouraged to supplement these with motion sensors on all the doors as well as a sensor on the floor next to the bed so that she can record her mother's wakings and movements throughout the day or night. These are all with the mother's acceptance which is an important recognition of her privacy. Her mom also is "open to" having a care manager drop by periodically just to check on her well-being. This is an important human complement to the technology which cannot see everything and surely does not process what is visible the same way a trained care manager can.

All of these steps are temporary stop gaps as the care receiver is still quite independent, although dementia places anyone at risk for elopement. Should that happen, Adult Protective Services could enter the picture and make very clear demands of the family to safeguard against the mother's wander risk. As with many conditions in their early stages, this now becomes a waiting game.

OUR TAKEAWAY: The professional Care Manager says that now may be the time to begin a conversation about a new residence in an independent living facility where services can be brought in for her mother as needed. Facilities often refer to this arrangement as sliding scale or ala carte. They will continue to provide assistance and security for the mother until the needs grow beyond what can be considered truly "independent" living. In our experience, facilities will often go the extra mile in order to have a satisfied resident stay in place with them. The exception will be when the resident poses a threat to themselves or to other residents. We suggest that there may be a step prior to even these. Assistance can be brought to an individual living relatively independently which could bring in or prepare meals, offer medication prompts or assist with hygiene or transportation.

Case Study 1.8

Lesson Learned: Get help for you.

- *Do not go it alone*
- *You do not have to be great at everything that needs to be done; delegate*
- *Care for the caregiver*

(ID: E43) The caregiver is the "new" 88 year old wife of a 94 year old veteran on disability with PTSD. The husband receives most of his care through the VA, but he has fallen as a result of his decreasing motor control, a concomitant of his dementia. The wife continues to attempt to care for him, but is overwhelmed, a warning sign of which is her falling behind on their bills and finances. The wife is in denial, seeing him as he used to be – and as she wants him to be - in his prime.

The first line of attack was to bring in non-medical home care for the husband on a recurring basis which also has the benefit of providing respite care for the wife. The home care assistant also was able to help him with bathing and other personal care which the wife simply did not have the strength to do. The husband initially resisted the assistance. The wife also failed to grasp the extent of his dementia, instead taking him along to her medical appointments as they had done before the onset. As a result he would leave the reception area of the office off wandering the halls of the facility where her physician was located...the facility management was unsettled.

To address the elopement and facilitate better care for the wife, additional hours of respite care have been a help. Even so, the saga continues. The husband has been recently hospitalized and subsequently discharged to rehab, but they both resist assisted living so they remain "independent." The new wife may have some cognitive issues of her own. Although the children of the husband offer their help, the help is not accepted.

OUR TAKEAWAY: There are a lot of "moving parts" here. It is an ongoing saga, and the complexity is compounded by numerous other family members attempting to "be of help." And the husband has been to no less than three social workers at the VA. Fewer players equals fewer complications. A series of family conferences ought to be held to discuss dad's health status and detail his needs. The wife's agreement and participation should be enlisted and possible extend this circle of conversation to her children, if she has some. This is because each of the partner's well-being affects the other, and the most affected children should be brought to the table.

Chapter Nine:

Resources for the dementia caregivers

Here are some of the national resources available to support the individuals who may need help when dementia rears its head:

1. **Alzheimer's Disease and Dementia Caregiver Center** is an arm of the Association that has done the most to help patients with the disease as well. The Center provides training and other resources to caregivers as well as a 24-hour telephone hotline. http://www.alz.org/care/alzheimers-dementia-support-help.asp

2. **Aging Care** offers answers and support from those caregivers who also are facing the challenges of caring for a loved one with Alzheimer's or Dementia. The site

allows you to "ask your questions and get helpful answers from caregivers, and memory care experts." They so offer a free guide, *"Life as an Alzheimer's Caregiver"*. The guide draws upon the experiences of elder care experts, caregivers to those with AD and patients themselves

https://www.agingcare.com/Alzheimers-Dementia/Questions-1

3. **Lewy Body Dementia Association.** We do not hear as much about Lewy Body Dementia (LBD) as we do Alzheimer's, but it is the second most common dementia diagnosed in America behind Alzheimer's disease. An estimated 1.4 million suffer from this condition whose hallmark is the presence of Lewy Bodies in the brain, protein deposits called synuclein. There are some treatments that have had a positive effect on LBD, but it is important to have an accurate diagnosis as LBD does respond differently than other dementias to certain treatments

https://www.lbda.org/content/local-lbd-support-groups

4. **National Institutes of Health.** The guide is specifically written for family members who care for someone with Alzheimer's Disease. It delves into how Alzheimer's Disease changes a person and how to understand and cope with these changes. It also offers practical advice on how to make home safe as well as how to plan for the future and get help or "shop" for an adult facility who can care for your loved one when the time comes.
https://www.nia.nih.gov/alzheimers/publication/caring-person-alzheimers-disease/about-guide

Chapter Ten:

Frequently Asked Questions – and their Answers

Here are some of the frequently asked questions we hear:

Do all people with dementia progress the same?

It is important to appreciate that there are about 100 types of dementia, Alzheimer's disease probably being the most recognized of them. And all of these nuances of neurodegenerative decline progress at least a bit differently from one another, so it is important to have an accurate diagnosis before one can begin to anticipate a "dementia trajectory." But even then, just as all individuals are unique and different, all people will respond to a given dementia in their own ways. We have addressed some of what patients and diseases within this category have in common, but they also have a lot of differences.

What kind of dementia does my loved one have; does it make a difference?

The type of dementia diagnosis is an important starting point. It will, in part convey a sense of the likely trajectory and sequence of deficits that are to be expected. It also dictates what kind of treatment can be brought to bear, if any. It may be your loved one's personal physician who brings the signs and symptoms to the family's attention. But an accurate assessment should include a neuropsychological evaluation, imaging, and even some blood or cerebrospinal fluid lab work. Once a work-up is complete, the consulting specialist can help prepare the family for not just the memory changes to be expected but also any other behavioral changes such as agitation, disinhibition or even depression.

What about what I have read about athletes developing dementia?

We have not addressed Chronic Traumatic Encephalopathy (CTE) or concussive-induced Parkinson's. In the case of CTE, it is professional athletes who have received repeated blows to the head who can manifest these dementias and often depression.

And we are now all reminded of the Parkinson's disease that afflicted the late Muhammed Ali. They are not tied to aging, per se. Parkinson's and Huntington's disease can both manifest dementia along with other neurologic symptoms, and we address these in the volume on chronic medical conditions.

My loved one is not going to remember any of this, but what about my feelings?

This comes back to the hard part of caregiving to an older loved one with dementia. It has to be about them, and not about the caregiver. Living in the moment is essential; this is when "now" becomes the focus, not the future. An older loved one with dementia will lose the ability to empathize and perhaps even recognize their caregiver, yet there will be moments that can be shared. Certain olfactory cues can bring back emotions and even happiness that can be shared. But the caregiver needs to take care of the caregiver. Support groups, friends and professional counselors should be part of the go to resources for a caregiver caring for a loved one with dementia. It begins with acceptance of the diagnosis.

Why is this happening to us?

Dementia is a feared diagnosis, because it robs the victim of their personality and their personal history. It also robs the family and the caregiver of a dear companion. While it is natural to respond with an anguished, "Why me?" It is more helpful to think in terms of "What now?" That is what this volume has been about. Caregivers to loved ones with dementia need to get educated about the specific diagnosis the loved one has been given. They then need to step up to identifying the resources that can be brought to bear to retain the greatest quality of life possible for the loved one, find out what is covered by health insurance and what is not and more. As important as any of that, however, will be a focus on caring for the caregiver throughout it all.

PART THREE:

Caring for the Caregiver

"I went from five hours of uninterrupted sleep a night caring for my mother in the house to five hours of interrupted sleep a night."
~Anonymous Caregiver

Chapter Eleven:
How to Love Yourself and Your Care Receiver

We both had the good fortune to have attended a business coaching seminar recently. The coach was very clear in stating that unless you make it a priority, unless you consistently work on it, you will not be successful. Sounds like good business advice, right? Well, it was advice the coach followed on how to make physical workouts a priority so that she could be energized to work on the business of doing business.

> ***You, the caregiver, must make you a priority...or you will not be able to care for your loved one.***

This, from a coach who had neglected herself for years, but with the realization that her health and her body needed to be a priority, she was able to not only shed over fifty pounds, but also found her hours working on the business were more productive. The hours spent in physically working her body gave her a much clearer mental grasp of her business priorities and the energy to execute. She had learned that taking care of herself was a huge part of taking care of her business.

In our personal and professional experiences, those caregivers who take better care of themselves, whether that is a physical workout, a book club, a long walk or a conversation with a dear friend, also take better care of their loved ones who are their care receivers. So starting out with first things first: Who should attend to the caregivers? Clearly, part of the answer is the caregivers themselves. There are external supports that can be as basic as just giving a break to what some have characterized as "the 36 hour day" (book of the same name, authored by Nancy Mace and Dr. Peter Rabins) that many caregivers live. But this taking a break for the caregiver has become so central to care planning that it has gained a name. Residential and other facilities that care for older loved ones call it "respite care." It is not just taking care of the older loved one; it is giving the caregiver to that older loved one a break from the day to day stressors and responsibilities of active caregiving.

Chapter Twelve:

Recognizing the signs of caregiver burnout

Too many caregivers feel guilty if they are not there for mom or dad or for an ailing spouse 24/7. We encourage all caregivers to watch for their own burnout symptoms as a caregiver can only be as good for the loved ones who depend on them as they are for themselves.

> ***Stress is inevitable, but "burnout" is self-inflicted.***

Do you see the signs? Are you missing hours or days of work? Are you not able to track and pay all your bills...are you getting late notices? Are you not exercising enough? Instead, are you consuming a lot of unhealthy junk...sweets, fast foods, alcohol? Are you having nightmares or disturbing dreams? Are you feeling lethargic or maybe even depressed? Are you angered by minor issues, or are you impatient with your family or friends? Have you simply "let yourself go?"

If you can answer any of these questions with a "yes," you need to know that you would benefit from a break. There are resources and support systems that can help. Family, friends, volunteers, and care managers are all helpful. Getting your own support system or taking time out doesn't mean you are unsuccessful, not being a good daughter or son, or losing a battle, but it does mean you are getting through a very difficult and emotionally-charged time in your life.

One of our associates tells his story as one of a "slippery slope." What started as a call to his older mother while he was at the grocery store to see if there was anything she needed. It progressed to regular weekly shopping runs for mom and a fix it list for odd items around the house and then the trips along with her to the physicians' appointments. It escalated to the daily phone calls with questions or concerns and the almost daily errands. When his brother offered to take over while he took a week's vacation with his family, he reluctantly took the opportunity. On his return his brother professed that he could not have lasted more than that week.

> *If you are feeling overwhelmed with caregiving, get a second opinion. Chances are that you are!*

The first brother reluctantly agreed that he did not want to take up the reins again either. They found home care that gave mom the help she needed and gave them back their lives.

In virtually every community there are resources available to provide respite care. These will be independent or continual care facilities who offer day care for older adults while the adult caregiver/child is at work. Some offer care for periods that may range from days to weeks or even a month or more. If you are a caregiver, check into one of these local resources as a help in getting you through your week or maybe just a test case to see what difference this kind of help can make for both you as the caregiver and your older loved one.

To address or prevent burnout, consider the following:

- Become educated about your loved one's medical condition in order to be as effective as you can be.
- Recognize that you are not superman or superwoman; set some limits on what you and others can expect from you.
- Do not beat yourself up about feeling angry, afraid or even resentful; instead find ways to vent. Feelings are just feelings, no matter how strong they may be. Defusing their energy defuses their power and helps you to be more balanced.

- Talk is important, especially to a therapist or counselor or clergy member...even trusted friends as a principal way to vent.
- Lift smart. As a caregiver, be smart about not hurting your back when lifting, pushing and pulling; keep yourself in shape and use an assistive belt around your care receiver if your physician recommends it.

Appreciate that caregiving is a job, and that all jobs allow one to "punch out" from work as well as take vacations and breaks. Give yourself permission to take a respite from caregiving.

Most states have Agencies on Aging, such as in our own state, the Illinois Agency on Aging. Their mission is "to serve and advocate for older Illinoisans and their caregivers." http://www.state.il.us/aging/

Also, check on-line with the Caregiver Action Network. They serve a "broad spectrum of family members ranging from the parents of children with special needs, to the families and friends of wounded soldiers; from a young couple dealing with a diagnosis of MS, to adult children caring for parents with Alzheimer's disease." You also are likely to find local groups by simply entering "caregiver support (name of your city, county or state)" in your search bar. http://www.nfcacares.org/

You have probably heard for any number of health conditions that prevention is more effective than a cure, and this is as true of caregiving as it is for medical diagnoses.

> ***Caregiver burden is a condition that is better prevented than cured.***

When we are working alongside a family member who shoulders a big share of the care for an older loved one, these caregivers sometimes try to hide what they are feeling as a response to the stress of their physical and emotional workload. They are on a slippery slope from the stress of caring for a loved one to the burnout that can follow.

It is really important to distinguish stress from burnout. Experiencing stress is not the same as burnout, although stress that is not relieved can certainly lead to burnout. Here are a few contrasts along with some signs to look for in a family member who is the caregiver or even in yourself if you have taken on the role of caregiver:

- You are stressed if you are "hyper-involved," but burnout results in social disengagement from others.
- You are stressed if you feel in emotional overdrive, but burnout makes all your emotions duller.
- Stress can lead to anxiety about doing enough, but burnout typically results in depression.

- Stress can sap your energy, but burnout depletes your motivation and even your hope.
- Stress may induce a sense of urgency about all that you have to do, but burnout results in detachment or depression.

We have a client who is a husband caring for his spouse who has dementia. It is exhausting work, he admits, but he is quite dedicated to her. His response is to take daily breaks to workout at a fitness center in his residential complex. It gives him a chance to recharge as well as the physical capacity to do the next shift. One of our associates describes it as "taking care of yourself so that you are better able to care for another."

Check out some of the recommendations of a group called "HelpGuide." They sum up their approach in three R's:

- Recognize-identify the symptoms
- Reverse-address the stress and/or seek help
- Resilience-take care of your emotional and physical well-being.

  http://www.helpguide.org/articles/stress/preventing-burnout.html

From Burnout to Depression.

Caregiving has some obvious costs in time, money and other resources, but one cost that does not get enough attention is the toll it can take in the form of caregiver depression. As care managers, one of our principal points of contact is the member of the family who has been delegated or who has defaulted into the role of caregiver for an older adult or other person with special needs. And while we are all about the business of planning for the care receiver, it also is critical to address the individual who is providing the care. The sad irony is that the caregiver feels guilty about even talking about the dark cloud that may be hanging over them, guilty that they do not feel the fulfillment of taking care of the parent who once took care of them.

More than 20 million Americans suffer from depression, and caregivers are more likely than the average person to get something that is not just the "blues." We all recognize the time and work that a caregiver puts in to help an older adult, but what we may not fully realize is that they also may be giving up the time they would have been spending with their spouse or significant other.

Or the nights out with friends and acquaintances, the moments during any given week that would give a break from the routine, make them laugh or fulfill them.

> **_Caregiving can lead to depression,_**
> **_but it doesn't have to; you have a choice._**

Today's caregivers are part of the "sandwich generation" if they have not yet fully launched their children and they are also are still earning a paycheck. The paycheck comes with a host of time and task responsibilities and the expectations of bosses, colleagues and customers. Now, add to those the responsibilities and worries of caring for mom or dad and you have a recipe for depression.

If you or someone you know is a caregiver, we recommend the following strategies:

- Include you; make time each day to do something that delights, relieves or distracts you.
- Make lists; prioritize your caregiving duties, make lists and you will see you are making progress even when there remains more to do.
- Request help; appreciate that it is gratifying to the others whom you may ask for help to be of help to you and your elder.
- Leverage your abilities; the professionals who can give you respite are actually better equipped for what you may delegate than you are, a win-win.
- Just laugh; hard work like caregiving can seem devoid of fun, so you have to take time to giggle.

If you are a caregiver who has been feeling a bit "down" lately – or for a long while - we urge you to not just write it off as a "little sadness." Check yourself out, and if the results suggest you are suffering from depression then get help. You will be both better for yourself and better for your care receiver.

If you feel depressed, say something!

A web site called Psych Central has a screening checklist for depression. It is a website that has been run by mental health professionals. We add that taking a self-administered screening on the WEB is not a professional diagnosis, but it can be a useful indicator that action would be beneficial.

http://depressionscreen.org/depression_quiz_a.html

Check in with your physician if you are experiencing feelings of sadness, anger, exhaustion, etc.

You can request a referral to a mental health professional that will have the skills to help you address these feelings and better manage them so that you can feel more heard, understood, at ease, at peace, calm and settled. You will be a stronger you and a more effective caregiver.

Technology to the Rescue?

Caregiving in this century is not just handholding; it combines the latest digital tools with caring to allow almost anyone to be virtually anywhere they are needed. A study produced by a partnership between the National Alliance for Caregiving and United Healthcare offers results of a nation-wide online survey of caregivers who are leveraging their caregiving with web-based and mobile technologies. The survey was based on the responses of 1000 Caregivers at least 18 years of age, who provided at least five hours a week of unpaid care to an adult relative or friend and had already used some form of technology to assist them in their caregiving. To see the full report, please go to The e-Connected Family Caregiver: Bringing Caregiving into the 21st Century.

http://www.caregiving.org/data/FINAL_eConnected_Family_Caregiver_Study_Jan%202011.pdf

Here are just a few of what we think are their insights for modern caregiving. The survey asked these people to rate how helpful they found each of twelve different technologies to be. You may get some ideas for your own needs from their answers. The three "most helpful" technologies included:

- Health record tracking that would help the caregiver to follow their loved one's history, current status and other metrics even if they cannot be at all appointments;
- Shared electronic calendars to allow everyone to track a loved one's doctor appointments and other needs;
- Electronic reminder systems to help the loved one stay on schedule with medications as well as actually dispense the pills.

> *Technology will not replace "touch," but it can make it more efficient and effective.*

118

Although the most common challenge to using these and other technologies was their real or perceived cost, the greatest benefits caregivers see for themselves and their loved ones are, in order:

- Saving time,
- More easily managed logistics,
- Greater safety for their loved ones,
- A sense of increased effectiveness for the caregiver, and
- Just reducing the stress that a lot of caregivers feel.

So, what beyond cost stands in the way of caregivers embracing these new technologies and others? If you are like most caregivers, you want to be told about technologies from a trusted source like your physician before you will buy it. Or you want to actually have someone walk them through how the technology works. One of the clear themes to emerge beyond the value of technology is the basic fact that almost all caregivers already use technology in the form of Internet access.

Intentional Caregiving.

So, is there <u>un</u>intentional caregiving? The answer is "yes," and there is a lot more than you may at first think. We have all heard people use expressions like "I was so busy I didn't know which way was up." What they really may have been saying is that they got so caught up in the chaos of the moment that they were doing more motion than making progress. We wrote earlier of the "dementia of distraction." Well, that's a reference to the forgetfulness that comes from dividing our attention across too many simultaneous tasks. Life in the current high tech environment has us all stimulated by any number of people, things or gadgets. We are not going to recommend that caregivers unplug entirely from caregiving as some technology gurus encourage for those going through "tech detox" by simply disconnecting from all things tech periodically. Caregiving does not allow that, but intentional caregiving can be a way of engaging in what a Zen master might call "contemplative caregiving." Intentional Caregiving is the opposite of the overwhelming chaos that can be the caregiving that comes from doing everything that is in front of us, everything we are guilted into doing and not giving any thought to whether we are really getting done what needs doing!

Think about it __and__ Meditate about it.

Intentional caregiving is about recognizing that every task we set out to do for a care receiver is an opportunity to make choices that help us be centered, thoughtful, productive and on-task. By being more intentional we actually get more done with less ...less time, less energy and less anxiety. Here are some tips:

- **Keep it Simple:** Try to do a task or series of tasks individually. A Logical sequence would be nice, but at the very least avoid multi-tasking; multi-tasking results too often in every task being done sub-optimally.

- **Don't forget to Breathe:** We will get even more Zen than this, but appreciate that slow and even breathing is a way to give calming feedback to your brain. That feedback also helps to relax tension in the muscles. If you notice that your tongue is sticking out while you are engaged in a task, you are probably holding your breath. Breathe...

- **Try Something New.** Even caregivers are susceptible to the old adage: "If you keep doing what you always have been doing, you will keep getting what you always have been getting." Try new approaches, look for an app for whatever the task is, and maybe even change up the schedule a bit. Perhaps a hot shower at the beginning of the day is a way to soothe your muscles and refresh you mind before plunging into your chores.

- **Yes, Meditate.** This is the real Zen part. It is as simple as assuming lotus position...or anything that does not have your knees or ankles crossed and practice slow breaths ...in through the nose...out through the mouth. Repeat.

- **Recharge your Batteries.** We knew a caregiver who started out conversation by observing that he had gone from five hours of uninterrupted sleep a night to five hours of interrupted sleep. That is not sustainable. Seek out a professional care manager for local resources, check out respite care, get other members of the family...or the village...who can contribute. You need a break.

Ultimately, intentional caregiving is a win-win. Not only does the care receiver get a better outcome for whatever task, but you as a caregiver are taking better care of you.

Chapter Thirteen:

How to leverage caregiving with local resources

Let's repeat the larger lesson. From the perspective of care management, it is not just the patient with the condition that requires help; it is their families and other caregivers in their orbits.

> ***Going it – Caregiving – alone is not your best choice.***

Here are some more of the resources available to support caregivers who need help when they step up:

- Family Caregiver Alliance) offers families resources at the local, state and national level. Not all locales may be covered, but their information and other resources at the national level can be a real asset to families.

https://www.caregiver.org/national-center-caregiving

- **Rosalynn Carter Institute for Caregiving** offers training and education that go beyond just pamphlets. They do peer-reviewed literature searches across a range of related topics as well as sponsorship of researcher interventions that work. http://www.rosalynncarter.org

- **Philips Lifeline** is one of the longstanding names in home monitoring systems. It all started with "Help, I've fallen and I can't get up." But it has come a long way now with the same remote technology, but with interactive capabilities, GPS and more.
  https://www.lifeline.philips.com

- **ADT** has long been associated with home security, but that often translates into keeping "bad guys" out. Well, they have come a long ways now with monitoring that can allow a remote caregiver to an older loved one monitor when an older care receiver leaves the house. With video monitoring, it is also possible to see in real time just what is happening in the older loved one's home. They also have interactive monitoring capabilities for direct voice communication between a care receiver and a caregiver.
  https://www.adt.com/media/health

- **Veteran's Administration** is not a name one associates with proactive care for older adults. Yet, the VA has made great strides in recent years to recognize the aging population they serve. They have improved the healthcare available to older vets, but also the health education to help older vets maintain their viability and be educated on the foods that can help them to be the best they can be at every age.
  https://www.va.gov/GERIATRICS/Guide/LongTermCare/
  Well_Being_Eat_Healthy.asp

- **Medicare** starts with a 65th birthday. If your older loved one qualifies, the next step simply is to sign up. But it can get complicated from that point. Learn your A's, B's, C's and D's and maybe even more. Which of your loved one's providers actually accept Medicare is important is your loved one has modest financial means.
  https://www.medicare.gov/index.html

And more…

- **Medicaid** is where the state steps in. It is for the low income seniors who also will need Medicare, but will need more help. The most recent estimate suggests that just under 5 million Americans who qualify for Medicare will also qualify for Medicaid. It is the safety net that is there for your older loved one. It is very important, however, to own the process of qualifying, especially if your older loved one may need secure assisted living. Not all facilities accept Medicaid's level of reimbursement.

https://www.medicaid.gov/medicaid/index.html

- **EldercareLocator** is funded by the U.S. government and provides a unique matrix resource approach to resources nation-wide. From their web site you can search a range of service types by zip code to find specific services in your own city.

http://www.eldercare.gov/eldercare.NET/Public/index.aspx

- And, of course, the **Aging Life Care Association** helps visitors to their web site with a Care Finder that can be applied at the zip code level. If you reflect back on other historic public health challenges where cures ultimately have been found, they all started with building from the grass roots a support system that not only supported the patients but also the families. It takes a village.

https://www.aginglifecare.org

GLOSSARY OF TERMS

Activities of Daily Living (ADL) – refers to a quantitative assessment of how independently individuals care for themselves. There are a number of scales developed by professionals over the years, but they generally focus on some basic "domains" of daily activities that include eating, drinking, walking or generally getting about, bathing, dressing and toileting or continence.

Alzheimer's disease – is the most common form of dementia that affects memory, thought processes and behavior. It was first documented by Dr. Alois Alzheimer in 1906 upon autopsy of the brain of a woman who had manifested these behaviors. The changes in the brain can occur a decade or more before behavioral symptoms, and these changes include deposits of proteins from beta amyloid and tau tangles that result in progressive atrophy and shrinkage of the brain.

ApoE4 gene variant – Individuals with one copy of this gene variant can have as much as four times the risk as others in developing Alzheimer's disease, and two copies of ApoE4 increase the risk to tenfold.

Beta amyloid plaque – Because Alzheimer's is about the nerve damage in the brain, a cornerstone of medical diagnosis is the imaging of the beta amyloid plaque (protein fragments) that is deposited in the brain along with the twisted brain tangles that signify nerve cell death and brain damage. These are assessed by brain imaging – using magnetic resonance imaging (MRI) or computerized tomography (CT) scanning - and may be present long before any cognitive impairment is manifested.

Biomarker – Generally refers to a biological measure that is a consistent predictor of some biological or pathogenic process. When used in the context of Alzheimer's disease, medical professionals are looking for changes in key biomarkers, such as beta amyloid levels in the brain and blood glucose and glucose metabolic levels in the brain. What they identify as departures from the norm or from what are calibrated as healthy, they will carefully examine to see if Alzheimer's may have precipitated these changes.

Brain tangles – signify the nerve cell death and brain damage in the human brain that are the precursors of Alzheimer's disease. These are assessed by brain imaging – using magnetic resonance imaging (MRI) or computerized tomography (CT) scanning - and may be present long before any cognitive impairment is manifested.

Caregiver – typically is a family member or paid worker who looks after the needs of a sick, older or disabled person. This help most often is to assist with the activities of daily living that the care receiver can no longer independently perform.

Clinical trial – is an experiment or observation of individuals who receive an investigational therapy in a controlled environment where there most often also is a group called the control group of individuals who receive no therapy or a placebo. The extent to which there is a positive difference between the experimental and control groups can tell scientists if a therapy may be a successful in treatment in the population of affected individuals.

Cognitive testing – are used in assessing the brain's capabilities across a number of intellectual and sensory aspects. Results can help to identify more precisely what kind of deficits and therefore what kind of dementia may be affecting a patient.

Comorbidity/ ies – is / are the presence of more than one disease within a given individual. Common comorbidities include obesity and hypertension or diabetes and neuropathy, etc.

Congestive heart failure – is characterized by the heart's inability to pump as vigorously as it once did. This typically leads to a progressively enlarging heart as the heart works to compensate for its suboptimal performance.

COPD – this abbreviation for chronic obstructive pulmonary disease is characterized by an ongoing difficulty with normal airflow. It is the single term that now subsumes what were formerly called chronic bronchitis and emphysema.

CT scan – this abbreviation for computerized tomography scan uses multiple X-ray images in "slices" superimposed to offer a composite image that is more useful than simple two dimensional images.

Decompensation – refers to the deterioration of function of a body organ owing to ongoing stress, illness, tiredness or the aging process.

Delirium – an acute or transient state of confusion, incoherence or restless that may arise from infection, drug-drug interactions, surgery, lack of sleep, alcohol or other drug withdrawal. The onset is typically quite rapid (and this distinguishes it from dementia), but its duration is highly variable.

Dementia – is the overall term for a number of conditions that offer a decline in memory and other cognitive capabilities. It is distinctly different for delirium in that the onset is slower and takes place over time.

Depression – is a common, but serious, mental condition common among older adults. It is characterized by persistent melancholy, lethargy, irritability, loss of appetite and inability to sleep. It is not merely sadness.

Distraction – a diversion from that upon which one is focusing. It is used within the context of "dementia" as a constant product of our culture which diverts attention at the price of being able to focus or concentrate thereby mimicking forgetfulness.

Elopement – within the context of mental or cognitive impairment, it is the act of leaving a safe or secure place like home or other residence….wandering.

Executive function – when used in conjunction with brain function, it refers to the higher level cognitive processes that allow one to manage oneself and achieve goals.

Frontal lobe dementia – also referred to as frontotemporal dementia by virtue of the areas of the brain affected. It actually is a term that subsumes a number of dementias that affect personality, behavior and language.

Geriatrician – is a medical specialty that focuses on older patients and the conditions that are part of aging. It is distinguished from the field of gerontology by the M.D. that geriatricians have.

Gerontologist – a professional, sometimes a Ph.D., who studies the psychological, sociological and biological aspects of aging. Distinguished from geriatricians in that gerontologists are not medical doctors.

Grand rounds – the term originated with residency training in medical schools and is distinguished by its non-classroom approach to presenting actual patient cases for discussion, assessment and treatment planning.

Home care – typically refers to the services that can be performed in support of a person's activities of daily living, but do not include administration of medicines, diagnoses, etc. The activities of daily living for which assistance may be offered typically include food preparation, ambulating, toileting, dressing, etc.

Home health care – extends beyond the normal activities of daily living and may include administration of medications, blood draws, vaccinations, blood pressure readings, etc. These activities typically are performed by a Licensed Practical Nurse (LPN) or a Registered Nurse (RN).

Huntington's disease – is a genetically-inherited, adult onset disease that manifests itself in a neurodegenerative progression with movement compromise, cognitive and psychiatric decline.

Lewy Body disease – is the second most common dementia after Alzheimer's disease which is characterized by a decline in thinking, memory and language capabilities and the presence of proteins in the brain that are termed Lewy Bodies. It is challenging to diagnose, because the symptoms resemble other dementias.

Medicaid – is a federally-mandated program to assist low-income individuals in paying for health-related costs. It is funded by both the federal government and state government and therefore varies by state.

Medicare – is a federally-funded insurance program in two parts (A and B) administered by the Social Security

Administration for adults 65 years of age and older. Younger individuals with disabilities may also qualify.

MRI – MRI stands for Magnetic Resonance Imaging. Unlike X-rays, it is a diagnostic imaging technique that uses magnetic fields and radio waves to render a detailed image of the body's soft and hard tissues.

Neurodegenerative – a progressive loss of function in neurons that ultimately result in death of the neurons. It covers a broad category of conditions that affect not only the brain, but also the nervous system and spinal cord.

Neurologist – A medical doctor whose residency training has focused on the diagnosis and treatment of conditions affecting the central nervous system.

Neuro-psych evaluation – an evaluation of how one's brain functions making use of a variety of memory and cognitive processing tests that typically are administered using pencil and paper.

Neuroprotective – actions or pharmacologic interventions that serve to protect and preserve the integrity and functioning of neurons.

Neuropsychologist – a psychologist who specializes in the understanding of how the physical brain affects actual behavior. Such individuals are not medical doctors.

Non-medical home care – see "home care" above.

Nutraceutical – is a food or dietary supplement that is believed to confer a particular health benefit beyond just nutrition.

Parkinson's disease – a progressive degenerative disease of the central nervous system whose signs and symptoms include tremors and episodic muscular rigidity. It is linked to a deficiency of the neurotransmitter dopamine.

Power of Attorney (POA) finance – a legally binding document that gives person (referred to as the "agent" or "attorney in fact" permission or power to act on behalf of an individual in matters of property or finance.

Power of Attorney (POA) healthcare - a legally binding document that gives another person power to act on behalf of an individual in matters of medical treatment. The "power" typically is treated when it is deemed the person in question can no longer act for themselves or if they are not conscious.

Practitioner Orders for Life-Sustaining Treatment (POLST) – a document that varies somewhat state by state that specifies in advance what measures an individual wishes to have occurred in the event they cannot expressly grant permission themselves. These orders typically revolve around life-saving measures; they are sometimes referred to as advanced directives and are placed in a patient's medical files.

Presenteeism – a term used in human resource circles to refer to the net result of distractions of non-work issues to the employee on the job. It is compared with "absenteeism."

134

Protein tau tangles – Protein tau helps transport nutrients in healthy brain cells, but when tangles begin to form the transport system is disrupted. All brains have some tangles, but Alzheimer's patients develop far more of them as precursors to the onset of the memory issues that are the hallmarks of the disease.

Saturated fat – is found in relatively high concentrations in meats, dairy fat and eggs. It is associated with the LDL (low Density lipids) or bad cholesterol that is associated with cardiovascular disease.

Unsaturated fat – a fat that typically comes from plants such as olive, corn, safflower, sunflower and soybean. It is healthier, because it tends to not form "bad cholesterol" in the body

Transient ischemic attack (TIA) – also called "mini-stroke" it is a neurological event with all the signs and symptoms of stroke, but goes away within 24 hours. It is due to an inadequate flow of blood and oxygen to a part of the brain.

Vascular dementia – is the second most common form of dementia and is caused by a reduced blood flow to parts of the brain. Any given stroke event may go unnoticed, but the cumulative effect results in memory loss, confusion or other effects on executive function or motor ability.

SUGGESTED READINGS

- Boss, Pauline. **Loving Someone Who Has Dementia.** San Francisco, CA: Jossey-Bass; 2011.
- Coste, Joanne Koenig. **Learning to Speak Alzheimer's.** New York, NY: Houghton Mifflin Company; 2003.
- Cress, Cath Jo, Ed. **Handbook of Geriatric Care Management.** 4th ed. Burlington, MA: Jones and Bartlett Learning; 2017.
- Doukas, David and William Reichel. **Planning for Uncertainty: Living Wills and Other Advance Directives for You and Your Family.** Baltimore, MD: The Johns Hopkins University Press; 2007.
- Ghent-Fuller, Jennifer. **Thoughtful Dementia Care: Understanding the Dementia Experience.** Amazon CreateSpace; 2012.

- Johnson, Kathy, James Johnson and Lily Sarafan. **The Handbook of Live-in Care.** Palo Alto, CA: Home Care Press; 2011.

- Howell, Carol. **Let's Talk Dementia.** Pittsburgh, PA: Hartline Literary Agency; 2015.

- Kuhn, Daniel. **Alzheimer's Early Stages: First Steps for Family, Friends and Caregivers.** Alameda, CA: Hunter House Inc.; 2003.

- Loverde, Joy. **The Complete Eldercare Planner.** New, NY: Hyperion; 1997.

- Mace, Nancy and Peter Rabins. **The 36-Hour Day.** 5th ed. Baltimore, MD: The Johns Hopkins University Press; 2006.

- McGraw, Phil. **Real Life: Preparing for the Seven Most Challenging Days of Your Life.** New York, NY: Free Press; 2008.

- Peck, Kerry and Rick Law. **Alzheimer's and the Law: Counseling Clients with Dementia and their Families.** Chicago, IL: American Bar Association; 2013.

- Pritkin, Enid and Trudy Reece. **Parentcare Survival Guide.** Hauppage, NY: Barron's Educational Series, Inc.; 1993.

- Wayman, Laura. **A Loving Approach to Dementia Care.** Baltimore, MD: The Johns Hopkins University Press; 2011.

- Williams, Mark. **The American Geriatrics Society's Complete Guide to Aging and Health.** New York, NY: Harmony Books; 1995.
- Williams, Mark. **The Art and Science of Aging Well.** Chapel Hill, NC: The University of North Carolina Press; 2016

ACKNOWLEDGEMENTS

Life crises don't make appointments; they just show up. And for most people that means addressing a crisis with no experience and no plan. (Hope is not a plan.) If your family crisis has dementia at its core, this book may be the resource for which you have been looking....*your caregiver's coping companion.*

A resource like this one is not the brainchild of any one person. In fact, it is not the brainchild of just we two authors. We have been struck throughout our own careers with how hugely variable every family's experience with dementia can be, so just another book on "our journey with dementia" seemed just too narrow. So, we thank the many families who over the years have come to us to seek our perspectives, advice and help in their own families' journeys with dementia. While it was their journeys, it was our responsibilities to be the option-makers for the decision-makers. We traveled together with them.

We thank the team at our office who offer their constant flow of input and insights to our clients and to us: Gregory Peebles, Amy Portz, Karen LaBranche and LeAnn Gannon. We also were struck with how beneficial it always has been when we gather or get on conference calls with other professional care managers and share experiences. So we need to thank those care managers who are our peers as well as the three dozen professional care managers whom we interviewed and who did "grand rounds" with us, sharing 70 case studies of families whom they have counseled on their own journeys with dementia.

This book represents the sum total of our training, our client engagements and also the numerous case studies from which we have distilled what we believe to be the important lessons learned. We share all of this with the reader suddenly immersed in what may seem a very frightening, confusing and potentially overwhelming crisis and life journey with dementia.

This book is just one in our **Caregivers' Coping Companion** Series. As we underscore in Part One, most family crises are more than one issue...more like five crises at once. Feel free to consult our other books on the other crises families face. Please also follow this link to Charlotte's Blog, a searchable resource with more than 500 postings:

https://creativecaremanagement.com/senior-care-blog/

Please send your questions to:

info@creativecaremanagement.com

Made in the USA
San Bernàrdino, CA
24 January 2018